THE CAROLINAS

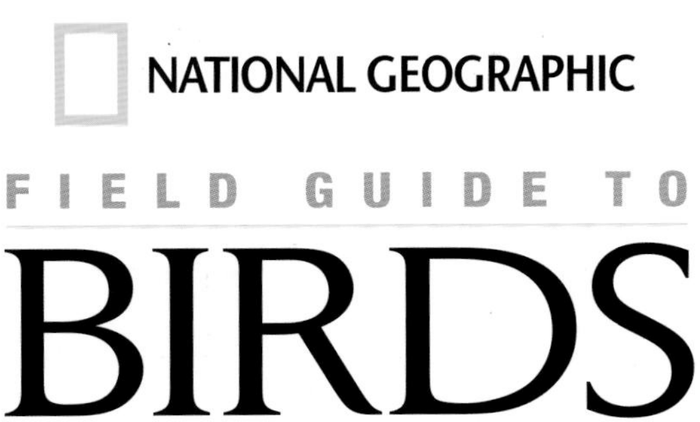

Edited by JONATHAN ALDERFER

National Geographic
Washington, D.C.

Introduction

The Carolinas host some of the richest bird life in North America due to diverse landforms, vegetation, and climate. Landforms range from mountain forests in western North Carolina to low country in coastal South Carolina. Varied habitat is key to the abundant bird life found here. One can expect to find most of the birds of eastern North America throughout the seasons of the Carolinas.

Most major plantlife of eastern North America is found in the Carolinas too. Western North Carolina's high peaks rise into the southern Appalachians. Here you will find spruce-fir forests similar to those of Canada. Some birds found in this habitat are at the southern limit of their range. The piedmont, sandhills, and coastal plain share a great variety of wooded and wetland habitats. Coastal habitats include salt marshes, ocean beaches, vegetated dunes, rock jetties, and offshore waters. The proximity of the Gulf Stream and the Continental Shelf, as well as the Labrador Current, make the waters off the Outer Banks a great environment for seabirding throughout the year. Some of the top birding sites of eastern North America include the Outer Banks and Huntington Beach State Park. They offer some truly terrific birding year-round.

The Carolinas have a rich ornithological history as well. Many well-known ornithologists spent time exploring the Carolinas and added much to the early knowledge of our bird life. Arthur T. Wayne, an early Carolina ornithologist, stated that more birds were first discovered in South Carolina than from any other state. Discovery continues today as present-day birders explore the Carolinas. Whether you are enjoying birds in your own backyard or at one of the many popular birding sites, you'll have plenty of places to go and plenty to see here in the Carolinas.

Lex Glover
South Carolina Department of Natural Resources

Frontispiece: Male Wood Duck Displaying
Photo by Tom Vezo

CONTENTS

SELECTED BIRDING SITES OF THE CAROLINAS

APPALACHIAN MOUNTAINS
BLUE RIDGE
TENNESSEE
NEW RIVER S.P.
Yadkin
GREAT SMOKY MOUNTAINS NATIONAL PARK
PISGAH N.F.
PISGAH N.F.
Winston-Salem
Greensboro
Catawba
Lake Norman
NORTH
Fontana Lake
PISGAH N.F.
Jackson Park
UWHARRIE N.F.
NANTAHALA N.F.
Hendersonville
Charlotte
CAESARS HEAD S.P.
TABLE ROCK S.P.
Wylie Lake
Broad
PEE DEE N.W.R.
Walhalla State Fish Hatchery
SUMTER N.F.
Hartwell Lake
Catawba
CAROLINA SANDHILLS N.W.R.
SUMTER NATIONAL FOREST
Wateree Lake
PIEDMONT
Great
Richard B. Russell Lake
Saluda
SOUTH
L. Murray
Columbia
Lynches
Congaree
J. Strom Thurmond Reservoir
SUMTER NATIONAL FOREST
CONGAREE N.P.
CAROLINA
SANTEE N.W.R.
Santee
Orangeburg
L. Marion
GEORGIA
L. Moultrie
Francis Beidler Forest
Savannah
Edisto
Charleston
Webb Wildlife Center
Garnett
ACE BASIN N.W.R.
PINCKNEY ISLAND N.W.R.
Sea Isl
SAVANNAH N.W.R.
Port Royal Sound

miles
0 50 100
0 50 100
kilometers

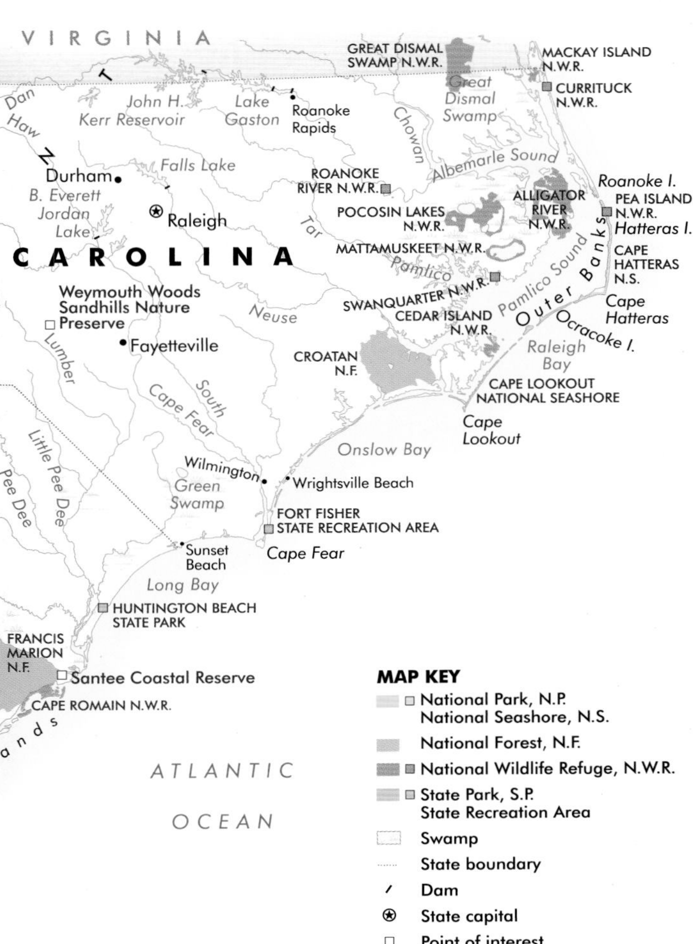
VIRGINIA
CAROLINA
GREAT DISMAL SWAMP N.W.R.
Great Dismal Swamp
MACKAY ISLAND N.W.R.
CURRITUCK N.W.R.
Dan
Haw
John H. Kerr Reservoir
Lake Gaston
Roanoke Rapids
Chowan
Albemarle Sound
Falls Lake
Durham
B. Everett Jordan Lake
Raleigh
ROANOKE RIVER N.W.R.
Tar
POCOSIN LAKES N.W.R.
ALLIGATOR RIVER N.W.R.
Roanoke I.
PEA ISLAND N.W.R.
Hatteras I.
CAPE HATTERAS N.S.
MATTAMUSKEET N.W.R.
Pamlico
Pamlico Sound
Outer Banks
SWANQUARTER N.W.R.
CEDAR ISLAND N.W.R.
Cape Hatteras
Ocracoke I.
Weymouth Woods Sandhills Nature Preserve
Neuse
Fayetteville
Lumber
CROATAN N.F.
Raleigh Bay
CAPE LOOKOUT NATIONAL SEASHORE
Cape Lookout
South
Cape Fear
Onslow Bay
Little Pee Dee
Pee Dee
Wilmington
Wrightsville Beach
Green Swamp
FORT FISHER STATE RECREATION AREA
Sunset Beach
Cape Fear
Long Bay
HUNTINGTON BEACH STATE PARK
FRANCIS MARION N.F.
Santee Coastal Reserve
CAPE ROMAIN N.W.R.
ands
ATLANTIC OCEAN
MAP KEY
National Park, N.P.
National Seashore, N.S.
National Forest, N.F.
National Wildlife Refuge, N.W.R.
State Park, S.P.
State Recreation Area
Swamp
State boundary
Dam
State capital
Point of interest

Looking at Birds

What do the artist and the nature lover share? A passion for being attuned to the world and all of its complexity, via the senses. Every time you go out into the natural world, or even view it through a window, you have another opportunity to see what is there. And the more you know what you are looking at, the more you see.

Even if you are not yet a committed birder, it makes sense to take a field guide with you when you go out for a walk or a hike. Looking for and identifying birds will sharpen and heighten your perceptions, and intensify your experience. And you'll find that you notice everything else more acutely—the terrain, the season, the weather, the plant life, other animal life.

Birds are beautiful, complex animals that live everywhere around us in our towns and cities, and in distant places we dream of visiting. Here in North America more than 900 species have been recorded—from abundant commoners to the rare and exotic. A comprehensive field reference like the *National Geographic Field Guide to the Birds of North America* is essential for understanding that big picture. If you are taking a spring walk in the Carolina countryside, however, you may want something simpler: a guide to the birds you are most likely to see, which slips easily into a pocket.

This photographic guide is designed to provide an introduction to the common birds—and a few rare birds—you might encounter in the Carolinas: how to identify them, how they behave, and where to find them, with specific locations.

Discovery, observation, and identification of birds can be exciting, whether you are a novice or expert. As an artist and birder for most of my life, I know that every time I go out to look at birds, I see more clearly and have a greater appreciation for the natural world around me and my own place in it.

Jonathan Alderfer
Editor

National Geographic Field Guide to Birds: The Carolinas is designed to help beginning and practiced birders alike quickly identify birds in the field. The book is organized by bird families, following the order in the *Check-list to the Birds of North America,* by the American Ornithologists' Union. Families share structural characteristics, and by learning these shared characteristics early, birders can establish a basis for a lifetime of identifying birds and related family members with great accuracy—sometimes merely at a glance. (For quick reference in the field, use the color and alphabetical indexes at the back of this book.)

A family may have one member or dozens of members, or species. In this book each family is identified by its common name in English along the right-hand border of each spread. Each species is also identified in English, with its Latin genus and species—its scientific name—found directly underneath. One species is featured in each entry.

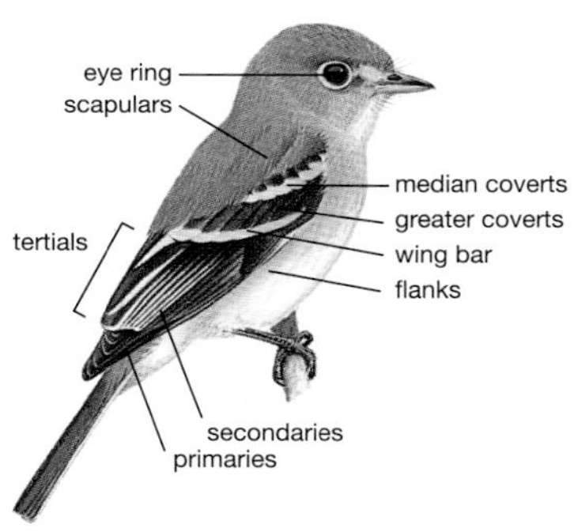

Least Flycatcher

Lark Sparrow

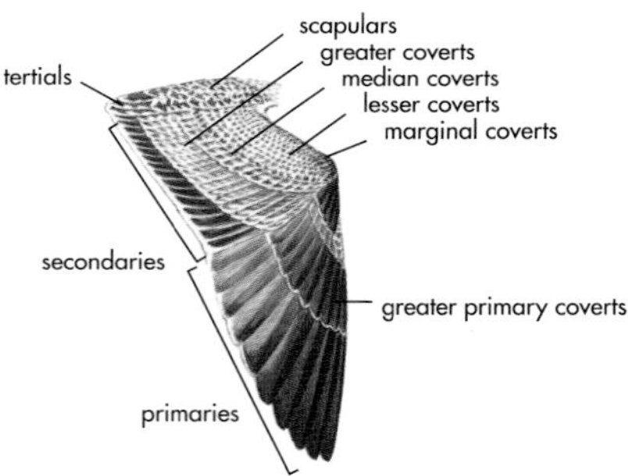

Great Black-backed Gull, upper wing

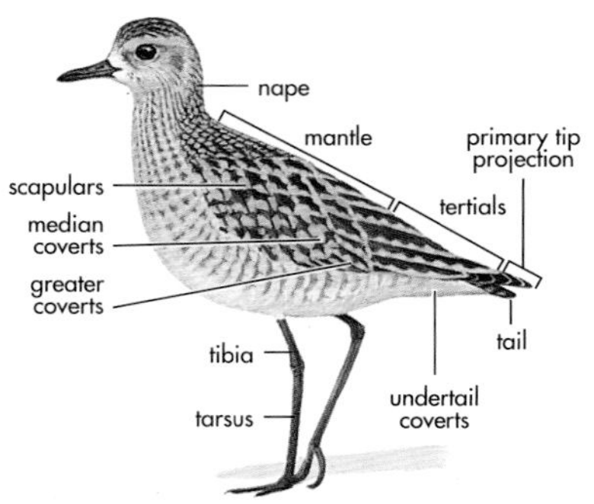

Pacific Golden-Plover

An entry begins with **Field Marks**, the physical clues used to quickly identify a bird, such as body shape and size, bill length, and plumage color or pattern. A bird's body parts yield vital clues to identification, so a birder needs to become familiar with them early on. After the first glance at body type, take note of the head shape and markings, such as stripes, eye rings, and crown markings. Bill shape and color are important as well. Note body and wing details: wing bars, color of primary flight feathers, wing color at rest, and shape and markings when extended in flight. Tail shape, length, color, and banding may play a big part, too. At left are diagrams detailing the various parts of a bird—its topography—labeled with the term likely to be found in the text of this book.

The main body of each entry is divided into three categories: Behavior, Habitat, and Local Sites. The **Behavior** section details certain characteristics to look or listen for in the field. Often a bird's behavioral characteristics are very closely related to its body type and field marks, such as in the case of woodpeckers, whose chisel-shaped bills, stiff tails, strong legs, and sharp claws enable them to spend most of their lives in an upright position, braced against a tree trunk. The **Habitat** section describes areas that are most likely to support the featured species. Preferred nesting locations of breeding birds are also included in many cases. The **Local Sites** section recommends specific refuges or parks where the featured bird is likely to be found. A section called **Field Notes** finishes each entry, and includes information such as plumage variations within a species; or it may introduce another species with which the featured bird is frequently confused. In either case, an additional illustration may be included to aid in identification.

Finally, a caption underneath each of the photographs gives the season of the plumage pictured, as well as the age and gender of the bird above, if differentiable. A key to using this informative guide and its range maps follows on the next two pages.

Reading the Spread

1
2
3
4
5
6
7
8
9
10
BROWN PELICAN
Pelecanus occidentalis L 48" (122 cm) W 84" (213 cm)
53
PELICANS
FIELD MARKS
Exceptionally long bill with dark gray throat pouch
Silvery gray above; blackish brown below; white crown; pale yellow forehead
Breeding adult's hindneck is chestnut; wintering adult's is white
Behavior
Dives from the air into water to capture prey. On impact, its throat pouch balloons open, scooping up small fish. Tilts its bill downward to drain water, tosses its head back to swallow. Sometimes gather in large groups over transitory schools of fish, attracting other seabirds to the feeding frenzy. Flocks travel in long, staggered lines, alternately flapping and gliding in unison. This formerly endangered species is currently making a significant recovery following a severe decline in its population due to pesticide poisoning.
Habitat
Largely coastal, the Brown Pelican makes its home along the shore in sheltered bays and near beaches. Breeds on islands in large stick nests.
Local Sites
Inhabitants of the Carolinas' coast, these large shorebirds can be spotted from sites such as Cape Lookout and Cape Romain.
FIELD NOTES The range of the American White Pelican, Pelecanus erythrorhynchos (inset), the only other pelican of North America, is currently expanding up the Atlantic seaboard. It can now be seen in winter in the southernmost coastal areas of South Carolina.
Breeding | Adult

❶ **Photograph:** Shows bird in habitat. May be female or male, adult or juvenile. Plumage may be breeding, molting, nonbreeding, or year-round.

❷ **Caption:** Defines the featured bird's plumage, age, and sometimes gender, as seen in the picture.

❸ **Heading:** Beneath the Common Name find the Latin, or Scientific, Name. Beside it is the bird's length (L), and frequently its wingspan (W). Wingspan is given with birds often seen in flight. Female measurements are given if disparate from male.

❹ **Field Marks:** Gives basic field identification for markings, head and bill shape, and body size.

❺ **Band:** Gives the common name of the bird's family.

❻ **Range Map:** Shows year-round range in purple, breeding range in red, winter range in blue. Areas in which a species is likely to be seen only in migration are shown in green.

❼ **Behavior:** A step beyond **Field Marks,** gives clues to identifying a bird's habits, such as feeding, flight pattern, courtship, nest-building, or songs and calls.

❽ **Habitat:** Reveals the area a species is most likely to inhabit, such as forests, marshes, grasslands, or urban areas. May include preferred nesting sites.

❾ **Local Sites:** Details local spots to look for the given species.

❿ **Field Notes:** A special entry that may give a unique point of identification, compare two species of the same family, compare two species from different families that are easily confused, or focus on a historic or conservation fact.

Reading the Maps

On each map of the Carolinas, range boundaries are drawn where the species ceases to be regularly seen. Nearly every species will be rare at the edges of its range. The sample map shown below explains the colors and symbols used on each map. Ranges continually expand and contract, so the map is a tool, not a rule. Range information is based on actual sightings and therefore depends upon the number of knowledgeable and active birders in each area.

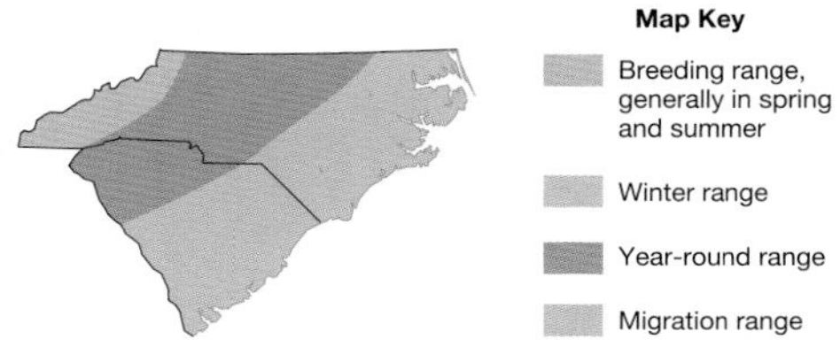

Sample Map: Blue-headed Vireo

Reading the Indexes

There are two indexes at the back of this book. The first is a **Color Index** (p. 262), created for birders to make quick IDs in the field. In this index, male birds are labeled by their predominant color: Mostly White, Mostly Black, etc. Note that a bird may have a head of a different color than its label states. That's because its body—the part most noticeable in the field—is the color labeled.

The **Alphabetical Index** (p. 266) is organized by the bird's common name. Next to each entry is a check-off box. Most birders make lists of the birds they see. Some keep several lists, perhaps one of birds in a certain area and another of all the birds they've ever seen—a life list. Such lists enable birders to look back and remember their first sighting of an Indigo Bunting or a Downy Woodpecker.

Year-round | Adult white morph

SNOW GOOSE

Chen caerulescens L 31" (79 cm) W 56" (142 cm)

FIELD MARKS

White overall

Black primaries show in flight

Heavy pinkish bill with black "grinning patch"

Juvenile is dingy gray-brown on head, neck, and upperparts

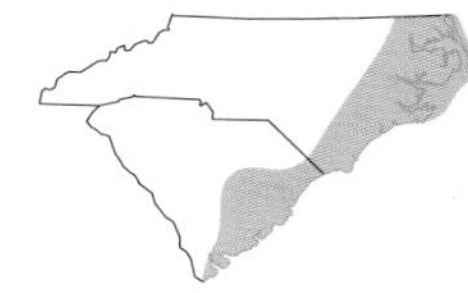

Behavior

Travels in large flocks, especially during fall migration. Loud, vocal birds, sounding like baying hounds, flocks fly in loose V-formation and long lines, sometimes more than 1,500 miles nonstop, reaching speeds up to 40 mph. Primarily vegetarian, forages on agricultural grains and plants and on all parts of aquatic vegetation. An agile swimmer, commonly rests on water during migration and at wintering grounds. Listen for its harsh, descending *wouk*, heard continuously in flight.

Habitat

Most often seen on grasslands, grainfields, and coastal wetlands, favoring standing shallow freshwater marshes and flooded fields. Breeds in the Arctic.

Local Sites

Found in winter along the length of the Carolinas' coast and on lakes and rivers slightly inland. Pea Island and Santee National Wildlife Refuges are two prime spots to scan for this bird.

FIELD NOTES Amid a flock of white Snow Geese, you may see a few dark morphs as well, characterized by a varying amount of dark gray-brown on the back and breast (inset). Formerly they were considered a separate species, the Blue Goose.

Year-round | Adult

CANADA GOOSE

Branta canadensis L 30-43" (75-108 cm) W 59-73" (148-183 cm)

FIELD MARKS

Black head and neck marked with distinctive white chin strap

In flight, shows large, dark wings, white undertail coverts, and a long protruding neck

Variable breast color, generally paler in eastern populations

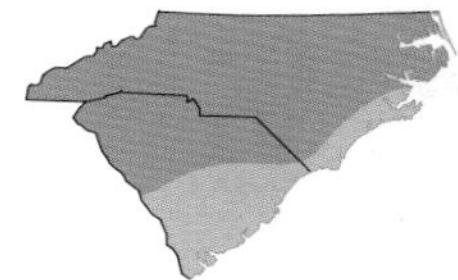

Behavior

A common, familiar goose; best known for migrating in large V-formation. Its distinctive musical call of *honk-a-lonk* makes it easy to identify, even without seeing it. It also makes a murmuring sound when feeding, and a hissing sound when protecting nests or young. Like many members of its family, the Canada Goose finds a mate and remains monogamous for life.

Habitat

Prefers wetlands, grasslands, and cultivated fields within commuting distance of water. Nests on the ground in open or forested areas near water. Has also adapted successfully to man-made habitats such as golf courses, landscaped ponds, and farms.

Local Sites

Look overhead and listen for flying V's, especially around dusk, year-round throughout most of the Carolinas.

FIELD NOTES Ongoing research into the mitochondrial DNA of the Canada Goose has found that the smaller subspecies, such as *hutchinsii* (inset, left) and *minima* (inset, right), actually belong to their own species, the newly named Cackling Goose, *Branta hutchinsii.*

Year-round | Adult

TUNDRA SWAN

Cygnus columbianus L 52" (132 cm)

FIELD MARKS

White overall with black facial skin

Black, slightly concave bill with yellow spot of variable size in front of eye

Juvenile appears darker with pinkish bill

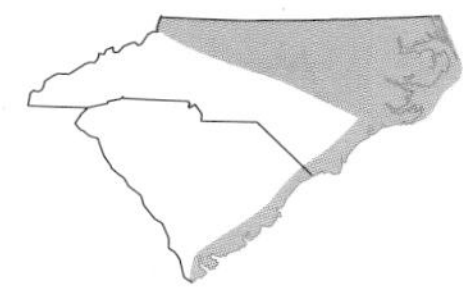

Behavior

Feeds on submerged aquatic vegetation in shallow water, using its long neck, which enables it to keep its body upright. To take flight, the Tundra Swan runs across water beating its wings. Flies in straight lines or in V-formation, with its neck protruding forward. Also an exceptionally fast swimmer. Call is a noisy, high-pitched bugling or yodeling, often heard at night.

Habitat

Winters in flocks along Atlantic coast on shallow ponds, lakes, estuaries, and marshes. Breeds on tundra ponds in Alaska and the Arctic.

Local Sites

Though you are liable to find Tundra Swans in winter anywhere waterfowl gather along the Carolinas' coast, Mattamuskeet National Wildlife Refuge near Pamlico Sound is a particularly reliable spot. It hosts tens of thousands of these birds between November and February most years.

FIELD NOTES By both day and night, the Tundra Swan migrates thousands of miles each year between Arctic breeding grounds and temperate wintering quarters, sometimes at altitudes up to 27,000 feet. Utilizing the same migratory routes year in and year out, it cuts diagonally across the interior of the continent.

Breeding | Adult male

WOOD DUCK

Aix sponsa L 18½" (47 cm)

FIELD MARKS

Male has glossy iridescent head and crest, lined in white; red, white, black, and yellow bill; burgundy breast with white spotting

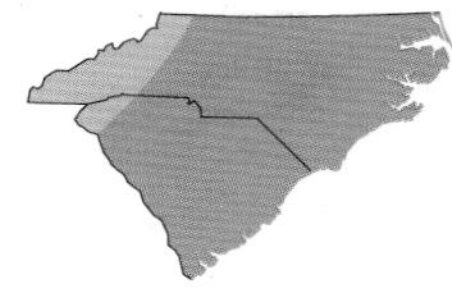

Female duller overall with large white teardrop-shaped eye patch

Squared-off tail shows in flight

Behavior

Most commonly feeds by picking insects from the water's surface or by tipping into shallows to pluck invertebrates from the bottom, but may also be seen foraging on land. The omnivorous Wood Duck's diet changes throughout the year depending upon available foods and its need for particular proteins or minerals during migration, breeding, and molting. Male Wood Ducks give a soft, upslurred whistle when swimming. Female Wood Ducks have a distinctive rising, squealing flight call of *oo-eek.*

Habitat

Prefers woodlands and forested swamps. Nests in tree cavities or man-made nest boxes. Will sometimes nest some distance from water if cavities are scarce.

Local Sites

Inhabiting wooded wetlands throughout most of the Carolinas, a pair of Wood Ducks may be as close as the nearest protected nest box.

FIELD NOTES The Wood Duck hen (inset) hatches up to eight eggs in cavities high up in trees or nest boxes. Once hatched, the young must make a long jump to the water, sometimes 30 feet below. Protected by their downy newborn plumage, they generally splash down safely.

Breeding | Adult male

GADWALL

Anas strepera L 20" (51 cm)

FIELD MARKS

Male mostly gray, with a brownish head and back, black tail coverts, and chestnut wing patches

Female mottled brown overall; dark upper mandible has distinctive orange sides

Both sexes have white belly

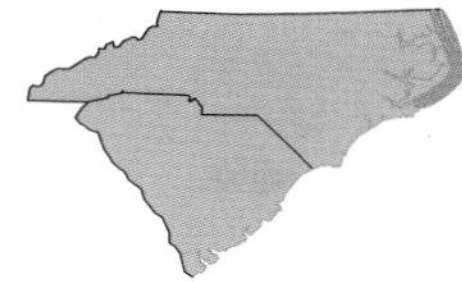

Behavior

Feeds primarily on aquatic vegetation, insects, and invertebrates in shallow water. Found in pairs or small groups, foraging with its head submerged, but without tipping up like many other dabbling ducks. Also known to dive for its food in deeper waters. Walks well on land, and may be seen foraging in some fields or wooded areas for nuts, acorns, and grain. Female's call is a descending series of loud quacks; male sometimes emits a shrill, whistled note.

Habitat

Uncommon in freshwater and enclosed saltwater habitats. Breeds in northern areas around the globe and winters southward from India to Africa to Mexico.

Local Sites

Though not as commonly seen as some of the Carolinas' other wetland inhabitants, Gadwalls can be found in winter wherever waterfowl congregate. Try the enclosed ponds of coastal sites such as ACE Basin and Pea Island National Wildlife Refuges.

FIELD NOTES Found throughout the world, but rarely in abundance, a number of Gadwalls were released by hunters in Long Island, New York, in the 1920s. The species has since gradually expanded its range throughout eastern North America.

Year-round | Adult male

AMERICAN BLACK DUCK

Anas rubripes L 23" (58 cm)

FIELD MARKS

Blackish brown body, paler on face and foreneck

In flight, white wing linings contrast sharply with dark body; violet speculum bordered in black

Male's bill is yellow, female's is dull green

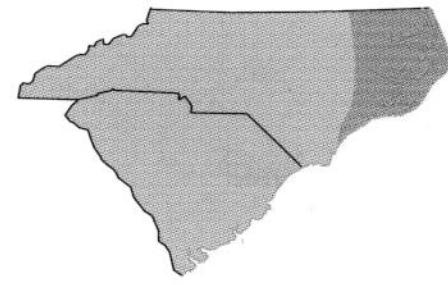

Behavior

Feeds in shallow water, mostly on aquatic vegetation in winter and aquatic insects in summer. If flushed, springs quickly into flight with no running start. The female Black Duck gives a typical loud quack, the male a lower croak. The population of the American Black Duck seems to be losing ground due to increased deforestation and displacement by the highly adaptable Mallard, with whom the Black Duck often hybridizes.

Habitat

Found in woodland lakes and streams and in coastal marshes, often in the company of Mallards. Female builds nest of plant material and downy feathers in a shallow depression on the ground.

Local Sites

Black Ducks can be found breeding at a number of spots in Albemarle and Pamlico Sounds. They move further south in winter when they are widespread across the Carolinas.

FIELD NOTES In coastal areas of South Carolina, the Black Duck is easily confused with the Mottled Duck, *Anas fulvigula* (inset). Look for the Mottled's unstreaked cheeks, paler body, and blue-green, as opposed to violet, speculum.

Breeding | Adult male

MALLARD

Anas platyrhynchos L 23" (58 cm)

FIELD MARKS

Male has metallic green head and neck, white collar, chestnut breast

Female mottled brown overall; orange bill marked with black

Both sexes have bright blue speculum bordered in white; white tail and underwings

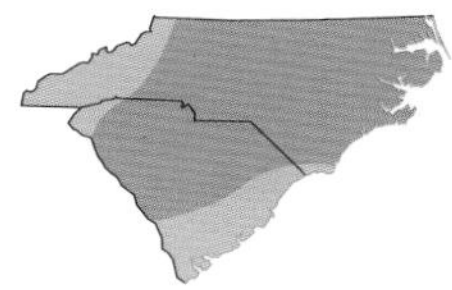

Behavior

A dabbler, the Mallard feeds by tipping up in shallow water and plucking seeds, grasses, or invertebrates from the bottom. Also picks insects from the water's surface. The courtship ritual of the Mallard consists of the male pumping his head, dipping his bill, and rearing up in the water to exaggerate his size. A female signals consent by duplicating the male's head-pumping. Listen for the female Mallard's loud, rasping quack.

Habitat

This widespread species occurs wherever shallow freshwater is to be found from coastal lagoons to urban ponds. Nests on the ground in concealing vegetation.

Local Sites

Mallards are the area's most abundant dabbling ducks. Look for them in lakes and ponds year-round throughout much of the Carolinas.

FIELD NOTES At first glance, the bright green head of the male Northern Shoveler, *Anas clypeata* (inset, right), can be mistaken for the Mallard's. Look for the Shoveler's large, dark, spatulate bill—a telltale mark on both the drake and hen (inset, left). The Northern Shoveler winters regularly on the Carolinas' coastal plain.

Breeding | Adult male

NORTHERN PINTAIL

Anas acuta Male L 26" (66 cm) Female L 20" (51 cm)

FIELD MARKS

Male has chocolate brown head; long white neck, breast, and underparts; gray back; long black central tail feathers

Female mottled brown overall

Long neck, slender body, and pointed wings evident in flight

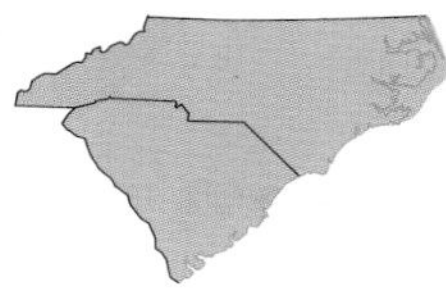

Behavior

Often seen in small flocks during winter months foraging for seeds in flooded agricultural fields or shallow ponds and marshes. Also eats aquatic insects, snails, beetles, and small crustaceans. This elegant duck is an accomplished flyer known for spilling out of the sky in spectacular rapid descents and leveling out directly into a landing. Male's call is a weak, nasal *geee;* female often utters a gutteral quack.

Habitat

Frequents both freshwater and saltwater marshes, ponds, lakes, and coastal bays. Also found in flooded agricultural fields, especially during winter.

Local Sites

Winter visitors throughout most of the Carolinas, Northern Pintails are most common along the coast at sites such as Santee Coastal Reserve and Pea Island National Wildlife Refuge.

FIELD NOTES The Northern Pintail hen engages in an elaborate in-flight courtship ritual in which the hen veers, swerves, and makes abrupt turns and climbs, challenging her suitor to match her moves. If he succeeds, she rewards the drake by allowing him to take her tail in his beak, or to pass below her so closely that their wing tips touch. If he fails her test, the hen signals to another drake to give it a try.

Breeding | Adult male

GREEN-WINGED TEAL

Anas crecca L 14½" (37 cm)

FIELD MARKS

Male's chestnut head has green ear patch faintly outlined in white

Female has mottled, dusky brown upperparts; white belly and undertail coverts

In flight, shows green speculum bordered above in buff

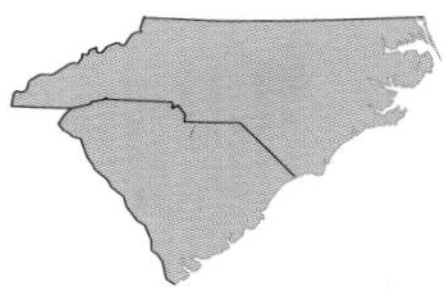

Behavior

An agile and fast-moving flier, this is the smallest species of duck known as dabblers. Dabblers either feed at the water's surface or upended, tail in the air and head submerged, to reach aquatic plants, seeds, and snails. The Green-winged has a specialized bill for filtering food from the mud. Travels in small flocks that synchronize their twists and turns in midair. The Green-winged hen emits a high, shrill *skee.*

Habitat

Found on coastal estuaries and tidal marshes, and on shallow lakes and inland ponds, especially those with standing or floating vegetation. Also known to feed in inland agricultural and wooded areas.

Local Sites

Like many of the Carolinas' wintering waterfowl, flocks of Green-winged Teals converge on coastal spots such as Mattamuskeet National Wildlife Refuge and Santee Coastal Reserve.

FIELD NOTES The Green-winged Teal hen (inset) is mottled brown overall with a small, dark bill. She can be told apart from other female ducks by her largely white undertail coverts and her green speculum, bordered above in buff.

Breeding | Adult male

CANVASBACK

Aythya valisineria L 21" (53 cm)

FIELD MARKS

Breeding male's head and neck are chestnut; back and sides whitish; breast and tail black

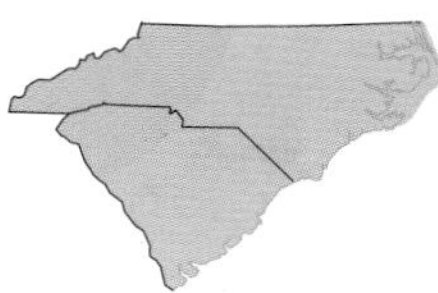

Female's head, neck, and breast are pale brown; back and sides pale gray

Forehead slopes to long, black bill

Behavior

Feeds on the water in large flocks, diving deep for fish, mollusks, and marine vegetation. Its heavy body requires a running start on water for takeoff. Flocks fly fairly high in lines or in irregular V-formation. Walks awkwardly, but not often seen on land. Listen for the male's croak and the female's quack.

Habitat

Uncommon in marshes, on lakes, and along shorelines, sometimes quite far out. Breeds in thick marsh grasses on upper Great Plains and north through Canada to Alaska, where it is a frequent victim of brood parasitism by the closely related Redhead.

Local Sites

Diving ducks, Canvasbacks can be seen in fairly deep water around North Carolina's Outer Banks. Look for them as well at more inland sites such as Santee National Wildlife Refuge.

FIELD NOTES Sharing the male Canvasback's rufous head and neck, the male Redhead, *Aythya americana* (inset), can be difficult to distinguish in the field. Look for its grayer back, its tricolored bill of pale blue, white, and black, and for its yellow eyes—the Canvasback's eyes are red. The two species share much of the same range and nesting locations.

Breeding | Adult male

RING-NECKED DUCK

Aythya collaris L 17" (43 cm)

FIELD MARKS

Male has black head, breast, back, and tail; pale gray sides

Female is brown with pale face patch, eye ring, and eye stripe

Peaked crown; blue-gray bill with white ring and black tip

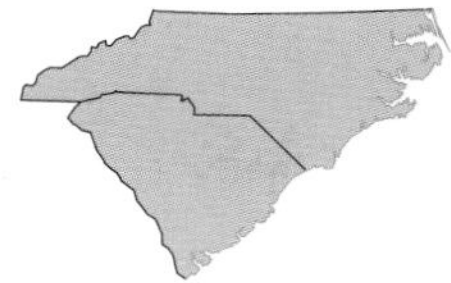

Behavior

An expert diver, the Ring-necked can feed on aquatic plants as deep as 40 feet below the water's surface, but regardless tends to remain in shallower waters. Small flocks can be seen diving in shallow water for plants, roots, and seeds. Unlike most other diving ducks, the Ring-necked springs into flight directly from water, and flies in loose flocks with rapid wing beats. Though often silent, the Ring-necked hen sometimes gives a harsh, grating *deeer.*

Habitat

Fairly common in freshwater marshes and on woodland ponds and small lakes. Also found in coastal marshes in winter. Breeds across boreal forests of Canada and into the northern United States.

Local Sites

Just as at home in winter on Appalachian lakes as in coastal salt marshes, look for Ring-neckeds on lakes, ponds, and marshes throughout the Carolinas from October until April.

FIELD NOTES The distinctive field mark that gives this duck its name is actually quite hard to spot in the field. At close range and with the right amount of light, you may be able to spot the male's fine ring of magenta iridescence (opposite) that separates his glossy purple head from his black breast.

Breeding | Adult male

LESSER SCAUP

Aythya affinis L 16½" (42 cm)

FIELD MARKS

Black head has a slightly peaked crown, sometimes purplish gloss

Black neck and breast, black tail; black-and-white barred back; white sides

Female has brown head, neck, upperparts; white at base of bill

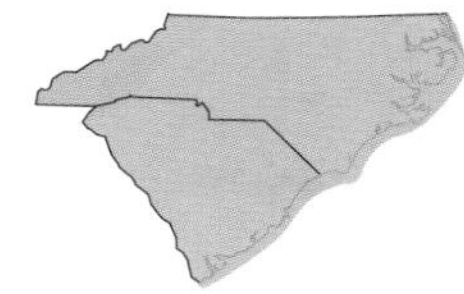

Behavior

One of North America's most abundant diving ducks perhaps due to its omnivorous diet, forages on aquatic insects, mollusks, and crustaceans. Will dive to bottom to sift through the mud while swimming. Also consumes snails, leeches, and small fish, and will forage for seeds and vegetation. Listen for the female's unusual rattled purr.

Habitat

Large flocks can be found in winter in sheltered bays, inlets, lakes, and rivers. May also wander inland to agricultural fields and marshes.

Local Sites

Though more common inland than its cousin, the Greater Scaup, Lesser Scaups still flock readily to coastal sites such as ACE Basin National Wildlife Refuge.

FIELD NOTES The Greater Scaup, *Aythya marila* (inset: male, left; female, right), very closely resembles the Lesser in both sexes. The Greater's more rounded head is its most distinguishable field mark. The larger amount of white on the Greater Scaup's wings is another helpful field mark. The Greater Scaup generally keeps to coastal saltwater environments of the Carolinas, while the Lesser is more likely to wander inland to freshwater lakes and ponds.

Breeding | Adult male

BUFFLEHEAD

Bucephala albeola L 13½" (34 cm)

FIELD MARKS

Small duck with large puffy head, steep forehead, and short bill

Male has large white head patch and a glossy black back

Female is gray-brown overall with small, elongated white patches on either side of her head

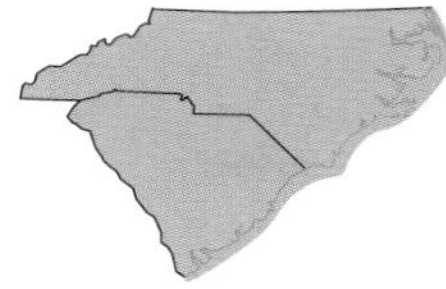

Behavior

Often seen in small flocks, some birds keeping a lookout on the water's surface while others dive for aquatic insects, snails, and small fish. Like all divers, its feet are set well back on its body to swiftly propel it through the water. Able to take off directly out of water, unlike many other diving ducks. Truly monogamous, Buffleheads are believed to stay with the same mate for years and to faithfully return to the same nesting site each season. Male's call is a squeaky whistle, female emits a harsh quack.

Habitat

Found on sheltered bays, rivers, and lakes in winter. Breeds for the most part in Canada.

Local Sites

Despite their diminutive stature, Buffleheads can be seen fairly far out in the open water off shorelines. Scan for them from lookouts at Huntington Beach State Park or Cape Hatteras National Seashore.

FIELD NOTES In its boreal forest breeding grounds in Canada, this smallest of North American diving ducks nests almost exclusively in cavities created by the Northern Flicker; a nesting site so tiny that it is speculated to have influenced the Bufflehead's own small size.

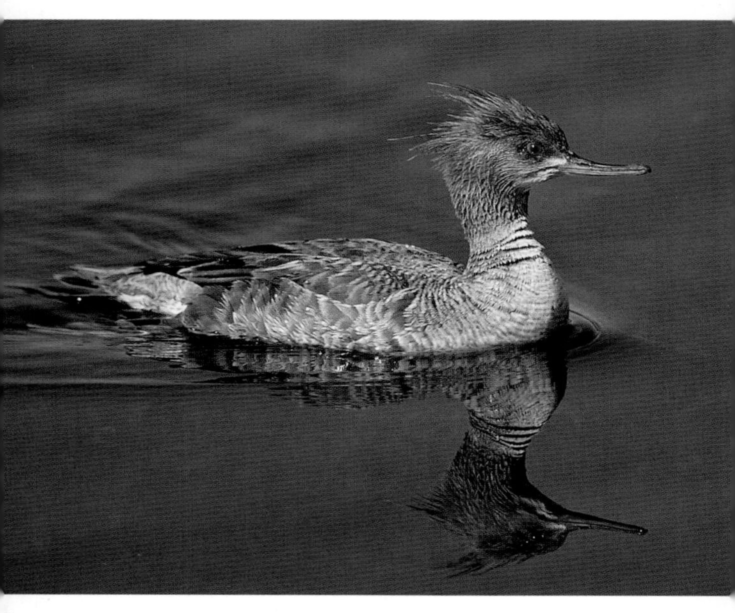

Year-round | Adult female

RED-BREASTED MERGANSER

Mergus serrator L 23" (58 cm)

FIELD MARKS

Male has a dark green head, a streaked breast, and a black back

Female has chestnut head, whitish chin and throat, and a gray-brown back

Both sexes have shaggy double crest and a red bill, hooked at tip

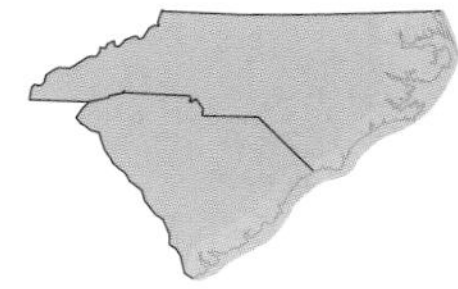

Behavior

Long, thin, serrated bill aids in catching small fish, the Red-breasted's principal food source. Flaps wings and runs across water or land to take off, but once airborne is a strong, swift flyer, attaining speeds near 80 mph. This merganser is a powerful swimmer using its rear-set feet to propel itself underwater. Often silent, the Red-breasted hen may sometimes utter hoarse croaks.

Habitat

Typically winters along the coast, seeking sheltered bays, estuaries, and harbors that provide calm salt water in which to forage.

Local Sites

Primarily a coastal bird in winter. Scan the shoreline and bay for Red-breasteds from Pea Island National Wildlife Refuge.

FIELD NOTES The Hooded Merganser, *Lophodytes cucullatus*, has in common with the Red-breasted a thin, serrated bill that aids in catching fish. The male (inset) has a large white head patch, conspicuous when his crest is raised, a white breast, black back, and chestnut sides. The female resembles the female Red-breasted (opposite) in her shaggy crest, but has an overall darker body. The Hooded Merganser is found in a variety of wetland habitats throughout the Carolinas.

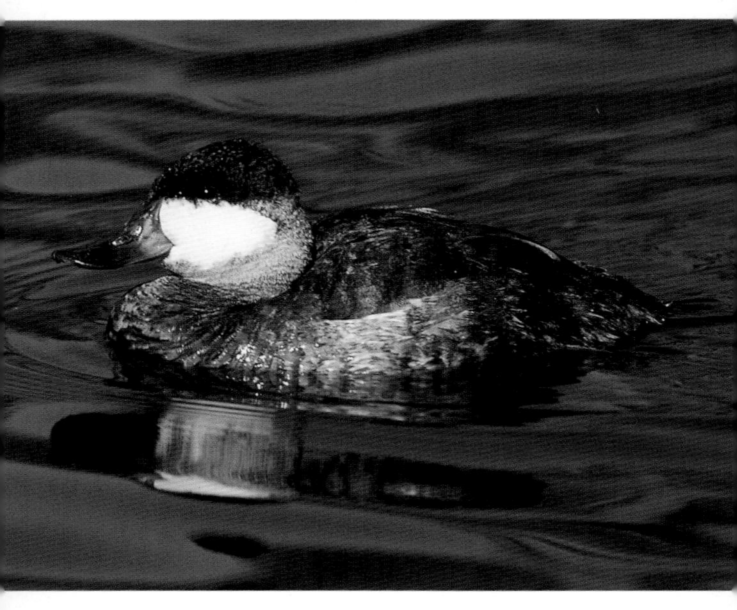

Nonbreeding | Adult male

RUDDY DUCK

Oxyura jamaicensis L 15" (38 cm)

FIELD MARKS

Brown-gray upperparts, pale underparts with brown barring

Male has bright white cheeks; female's cheeks crossed by single dark line

Breeding male has blue bill, black cap, and chestnut upperparts

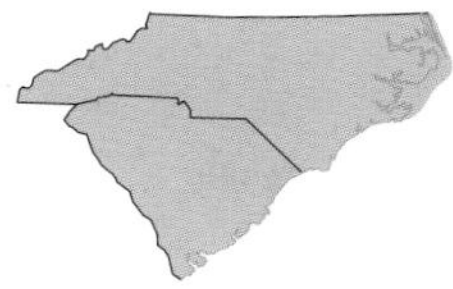

Behavior

Referred to as a "stiff-tail" from its habit of cocking its long tail upright, this small, chunky diver is noted for its grebe-like ability to sink beneath the surface of water and disappear from view, its stiff tail feathers serving as a rudder as it forages. Adapted for diving, its feet are the largest relative to body size of all ducks. With legs positioned far back on its body, it can barely walk upright. Feeds primarily on aquatic insects and crustaceans; eats little vegetable matter. The Ruddy Duck generally remains silent.

Habitat

Found in tightly clustered flocks on lakes, bays, and salt marshes during migration and winter.

Local Sites

Winterers throughout the Carolinas, Ruddy Ducks are found in greatest numbers coastally at sites such as Santee Coastal Reserve, Huntington Beach State Park, and Mattamuskeet National Wildlife Refuge.

FIELD NOTES One of the ducks most relegated to aquatic habitats, the Ruddy Duck, when disturbed, is as likely to swim away underwater as to fly off.

Year-round | Adult male

WILD TURKEY

Meleagris gallopavo L 37-46" (94-117 cm)

FIELD MARKS

Large land bird with purple, green, and bronze iridescent plumage

Unfeathered blue and pink head, red wattles

Male has blackish breast tuft

Female smaller, less iridescent

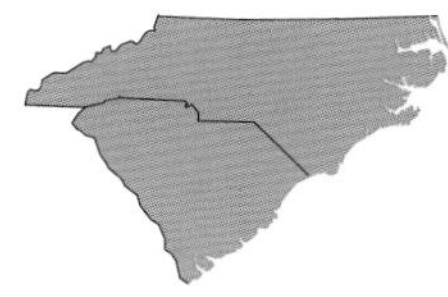

Behavior

A ground feeder by day, roosts in trees at night. Forages in open fields for nuts, seeds, fruit, insects, frogs, or lizards. It can fly well for short distances when alarmed, but prefers to walk or run. Male's characteristic display during breeding season involves puffing out his chest, swelling his wattles, spreading his tail, and rattling his wings, all while gobbling and strutting. In spring, male's gobbling call can be heard from a mile away.

Habitat

Largest of game birds, the turkey lives communally in small flocks, frequenting open forests and grainfields. Females raise large broods, nesting in leaf-lined hollows in brush or woodlands.

Local Sites

Since South Carolina's successful in-state relocation program of the 1960s, Wild Turkeys are widespread in open woodlands throughout the area.

FIELD NOTES The only other member of the family *Phasianidae* to occur regularly in the Carolinas is the Ruffed Grouse, *Bonasa umbellus* (inset). It is light brown overall, with a small crest and a multi-banded tail. In the Appalachians in spring, listen for the male's "drumming" display, produced by rapidly beating wings.

Year-round | Adult male

NORTHERN BOBWHITE

Colinus virginianus L 9¾" (25 cm)

FIELD MARKS

Mottled reddish brown quail with short gray tail

Throat and eye stripe white in male, buff-colored in female

Whitish underparts with black scalloping

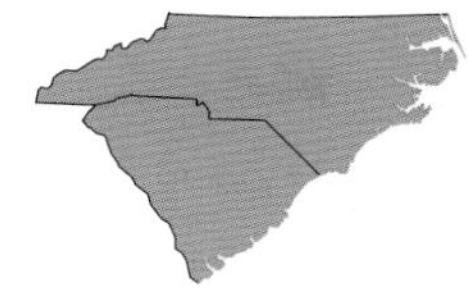

Behavior

A ground feeder, the Bobwhite forages for seeds, grains, insects, and leaf buds. Feeds and roosts in a covey except during nesting season. When alarmed, a Bobwhite is more likely to run than to fly. Male's call is a rising, whistled *bob-white*, heard chiefly in spring and summer. A whistled *hoy* can also be heard year-round.

Habitat

With the largest range of all North American quail, the Northern Bobwhite prefers farmland and open woodlands with plentiful underbrush. Nest is usually a woven cover of pine needles, grass, and vegetation with an opening on one side.

Local Sites

Though widespread, Northern Bobwhites are declining over most of their range. They can still be found in protected woodlands such as Francis Marion and Croatan National Forests, Carolina Sandhills National Wildlife Refuge, and Webb Wildlife Center.

FIELD NOTES To keep warm at night, a covey of Bobwhites, sometimes as many as 30, will roost on the ground in a circle, with heads facing outward and tails pushed together so that their bodies are in contact. Particularly sensitive to cold weather, entire populations can be lost in a single harsh winter.

Nonbreeding | Adult

COMMON LOON

Gavia immer L 32" (81 cm)

FIELD MARKS

Dark upperparts, pale underparts, white around eye in winter

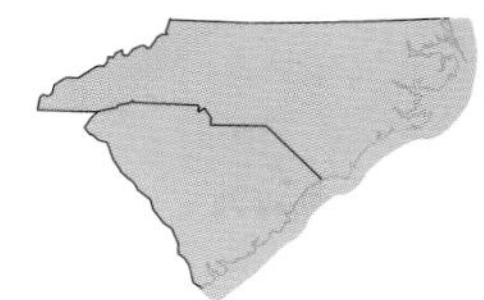

Blue-gray bill; slightly concave area between crown and bill

Dark on nape extends around sides of neck; white indentation above this

Behavior

A diving bird; eats fish up to 10 inches long, which it grasps with its pointed beak. Forages by diving and swimming underwater, propelled by large, paddle-shaped feet. Can stay submerged for up to three minutes at depths down to 250 feet. It is nearly impossible for the Common Loon to walk on land. Generally remains silent on wintering grounds.

Habitat

Winters in coastal waters, or slightly inland on large bodies of water. Migrates overland as well as coastally.

Local Sites

Scan the shorelines for Common Loons from lookouts along the entire Carolina coast. Inland lakes such as Falls Lake, B. Everett Jordan Lake, and Lake Marion also host a number of loons in winter.

FIELD NOTES The eponymous brick red throat patch of the Red-throated Loon, *Gavia stellata* (inset), is visible only during breeding season. In winter, in waters off the Carolinas' coast, the Red-throated can be identified by the sharply defined white on its face, which extends farther back than that of the Common Loon, and by its habit of holding its thinner bill angled slightly upward.

Breeding | Adult

PIED-BILLED GREBE

Podilymbus podiceps L 13½" (34 cm)

FIELD MARKS

Small and short-necked

Breeding adult brownish gray overall; black ring around stout, whitish bill; black chin and throat

Winter birds lose bill ring; chin becomes white; plumage is browner overall

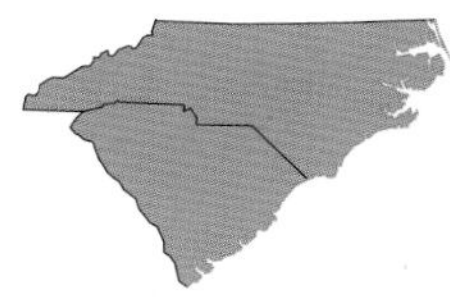

Behavior

The most widespread of North American grebes, the Pied-billed remains for the most part on water, seldom on land or in flight. When alarmed, it slowly sinks, holding only its head above the water's surface. Its bill allows it to feed on hard-shelled crustaceans, breaking apart the shells with ease. Pursues fish underwater and, once prey is grasped in its bill, will eat it whole while still submerged. Lobed toes make grebes strong swimmers. Call is a loud *cuk-cuk-cuk* or *cow-cow-cow.*

Habitat

Prefers nesting around freshwater marshes and ponds. Also found in more open waters of large bays and rivers, where it dives to feed on aquatic insects, small fish, frogs, and vegetable matter. Winters on both fresh and salt water.

Local Sites

Widespread throughout both states, Pied-billed Grebes may be found year-round on almost any body of water in the Carolinas.

FIELD NOTES Like most grebes, the Pied-billed eats its own feathers and feeds them to its young, perhaps to protect the stomach lining from fish bones or animal shells.

Breeding | Adult

BROWN PELICAN

Pelecanus occidentalis L 48" (122 cm) W 84" (213 cm)

FIELD MARKS

Exceptionally long bill with dark gray throat pouch

Silvery gray above; blackish brown below; white crown; pale yellow forehead

Breeding adult's hindneck is chestnut; wintering adult's is white

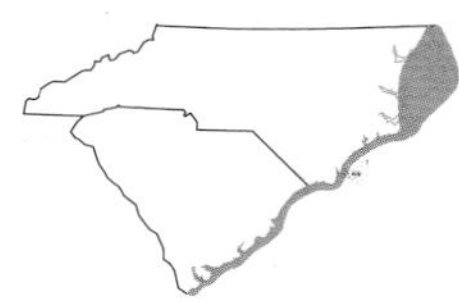

Behavior

Dives from the air into water to capture prey. On impact, throat pouch balloons open, scooping up small fish. Tilts bill downward to drain water, tosses head back to swallow. Sometimes gathers in large groups over transitory schools of fish, attracting other seabirds to the feeding frenzy. Flocks travel in long, staggered lines, alternately flapping and gliding in unison. This formerly endangered species is currently making a significant recovery following a severe decline in its population due to pesticide poisoning in the 1960s.

Habitat

Largely coastal, the Brown Pelican makes its home along the shore in sheltered bays and near beaches. Breeds on islands in large stick nests.

Local Sites

Inhabitants of the Carolinas' coast, these large water birds can be spotted from sites such as Cape Lookout and Cape Romain.

FIELD NOTES The range of the American White Pelican, *Pelecanus erythrorhynchos* (inset), the only other pelican of North America, is currently expanding up the Atlantic seaboard. It can now be seen in winter in the southernmost coastal areas of South Carolina.

Immature | 2nd Year

DOUBLE-CRESTED CORMORANT

Phalacrocorax auritus L 32" (81 cm) W 52" (132 cm)

FIELD MARKS

Black overall; facial skin yellow-orange; pale bill hooked at tip

Distinctive kinked neck in flight

Breeding adult has tufts of black feathers behind eyes

Immature has pale neck and breast

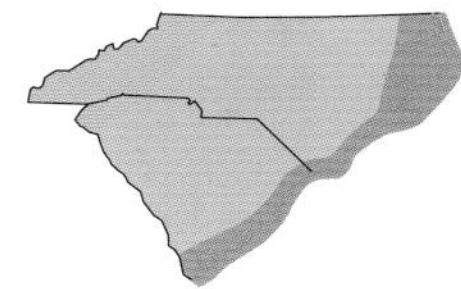

Behavior

After locating prey, the Double-crested Cormorant can dive to considerable depths, propelling itself with fully webbed feet. Uses its hooked bill to grasp fish. Feeds on a variety of aquatic life. When it leaves the water, it perches on a branch, dock, or piling and half-spreads its wings to dry. Soars briefly at times, its neck in an S-shape. May swim submerged to the neck, bill pointed slightly skyward. Emits a deep grunt.

Habitat

The most numerous and far-ranging of North American cormorants, the Double-crested may be found along coasts, inland lakes, and rivers; it adapts to fresh or saltwater environments.

Local Sites

Common breeders along the coast, Double-cresteds move inland in winter and are found on rivers and lakes across most of the Carolinas.

FIELD NOTES In summer, the Anhinga, *Anhinga anhinga*, joins the Double-crested in wooded swamps and ponds on the coastal plain of the Carolinas. Behaviorally similar, the Anhinga is distinguished by its long tail and by white streaks on its wings and back. Be careful not to confuse the pale neck and breast of the female Anhinga (inset) with that of the immature Double-crested.

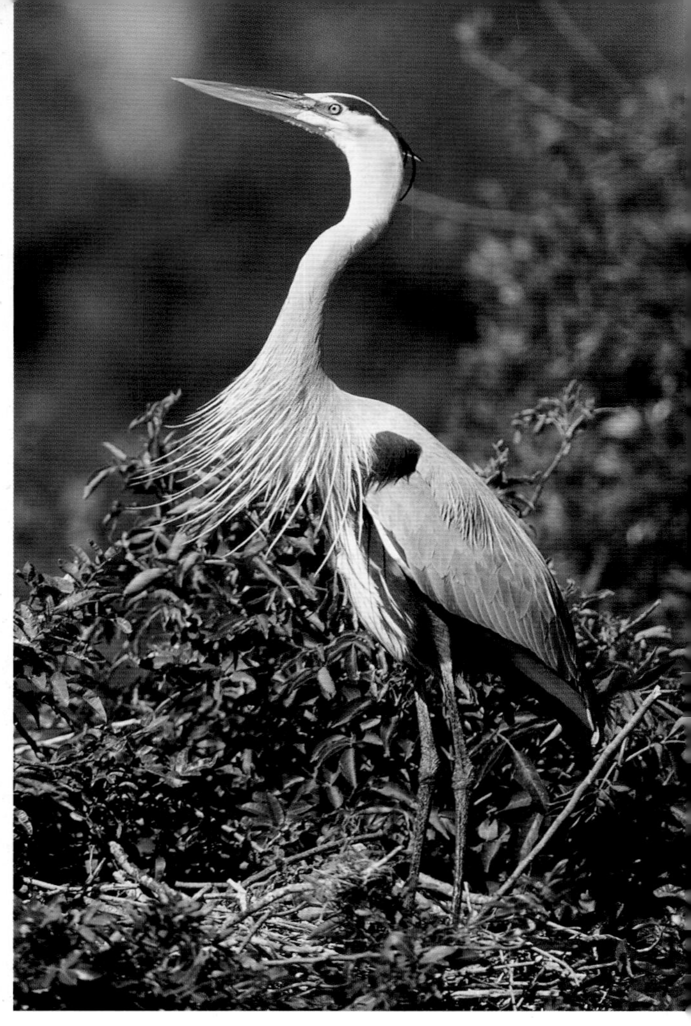

Breeding | Adult

GREAT BLUE HERON

Ardea herodias L 46" (117 cm) W 72" (183 cm)

FIELD MARKS

Gray-blue overall; white foreneck with black streaks; yellowish bill

Black stripe extends above eye

Breeding adult has plumes on its head, neck, and back

Juvenile has dark crown; no plumes

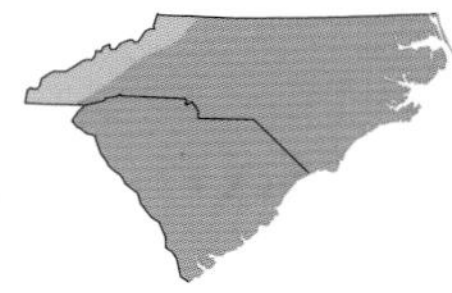

Behavior

Often seen standing or wading along calm shorelines or rivers, foraging for food. It waits for prey to come into its range, then spears it with a quick thrust of its sharp bill. Flies with its head folded back onto its shoulders in an S-curve, typical of other herons as well. When threatened, draws its neck back with plumes erect and points its bill at antagonist. Sometimes emits an annoyed, deep, guttural squawk as it takes flight.

Habitat

May be seen hunting for aquatic creatures in marshes and swamps, or for small mammals inland, in fields and forest edges. Pairs build stick nests high in trees in loose association with other Great Blue pairs.

Local Sites

Common and widespread, Great Blues can be found at a number of refuges along the coast in addition to just about any water source, lake, pond, or river, across the interior of the Carolinas.

FIELD NOTES The generalist of the heron family, the Great Blue feeds on fish, snakes, frogs, crabs, shrimp, and insects. Less tied to aquatic habitats than other species, it will also give chase to small birds, nestlings, or even small mammals, such as mice and woodchucks, which it often wets before swallowing.

Breeding | Adult

GREAT EGRET

Ardea alba L 39" (99 cm)

FIELD MARKS

Large white heron with heavy yellow bill, black legs and feet

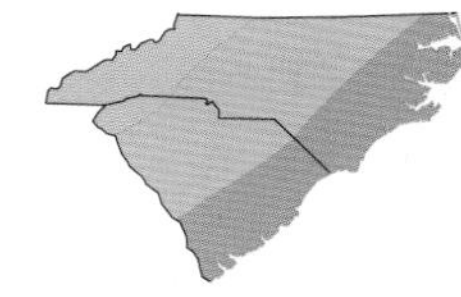

Breeding adult has long plumes trailing from its back, extending beyond the tail

Blue-green lores in high breeding plumage

Behavior

Stalks its prey slowly and methodically, foraging in shallow water with sharply pointed bill to spear small fish, aquatic insects, frogs, and crayfish. Also known to hunt snakes, birds, and small mammals. Occasionally forages in groups or steals food from smaller birds. Listen for the Great Egret's guttural croaking or its repeated *cuk-cuk*.

Habitat

Common to both fresh and saltwater wetlands. The Great Egret makes its nest in trees or shrubs 10 to 40 feet above ground. Colonies can have up to 100 birds.

Local Sites

Great Egrets can be found year-round in marshes and mudflats of coastal sites such as Santee Coastal Reserve and Alligator River National Wildlife Refuge.

FIELD NOTES The endangered Wood Stork, *Mycteria americana* (inset), often nests along with the Great Egret and other herons in colonies, such as ones found in ACE Basin National Wildlife Refuge in South Carolina. Roughly the same size as the Great Egret, this stork is distinguished by black flight feathers and tail, and an unfeathered, blackish gray head.

Breeding | Adult

SNOWY EGRET

Egretta thula L 24" (61 cm) W 41" (104 cm)

FIELD MARKS

White heron with slender black bill and legs; yellow eyes, lores, and feet

Breeding adult has upward-curving plumes on head, neck, and back; nonbreeding adult lacks plumes

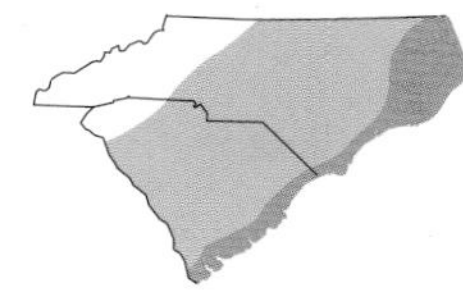

Behavior

An active feeder, the Snowy Egret may be seen running in shallows, chasing after its prey of fish, insects, and crustaceans. Also forages by stirring up bottom water with feet to flush out prey. In breeding display, the Snowy Egret raises its plumage, pumps its head up and down, and flashes the skin at the base of its bill, which has turned from yellow to vermilion. Also during breeding season, the generally quiet bird will bray gutturally, pointing its bill straight up.

Habitat

Prefers wetlands and sheltered bays along the coastline. Nests several feet up in trees among mixed colonies including heron, egret, and ibis species.

Local Sites

Look for Snowy Egrets almost exclusively at sites along the coast or in North Carolina's Albemarle and Pamlico Sounds.

FIELD NOTES In breeding season, the Cattle Egret, *Bubulcus ibis* (inset), acquires orange-buff plumes, easily distinguished from the Snowy Egret's stark white plumes.The nonbreeding Cattle Egret, seen in southern coastal regions of the Carolinas, is more easily mistaken for the Snowy. Look for its shorter, stubbier yellow bill.

Breeding | Adult

LITTLE BLUE HERON

Egretta caerulea L 24" (61 cm) W 40" (102 cm)

FIELD MARKS

Slate blue; dull green legs and feet; blue-gray bill and lores

Adult in high breeding plumage has reddish purple head and neck, black legs and feet

Immature bird white with gray wing tips, grayish bill and lores

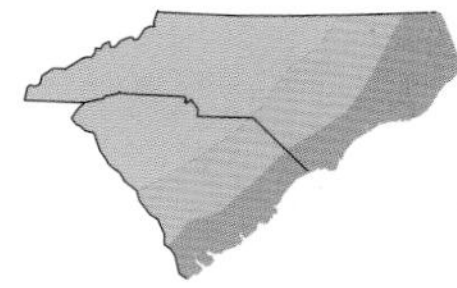

Behavior

A slow and methodical feeder, hunts for fish and small crustaceans. Strictly carnivorous, it snags its prey with its sharply pointed bill. Like all herons, the Little Blue may be seen preening its contour and flight feathers with its pectinate, or comblike, middle toes. Breeding male sings a distinctive *ee-oo-ah-ee-ee.* Both male and female emit hoarse croaks and squawks.

Habitat

Prefers freshwater ponds, lakes, and marshes, and coastal saltwater wetlands. Both sexes build nest of sticks and twigs low to the ground in a tree or shrub.

Local Sites

Little Blue Herons are most readily seen at sites along the Carolinas' coast, but they also disperse inland in spring to smaller freshwater rivers and ponds in order to find suitable nesting locations.

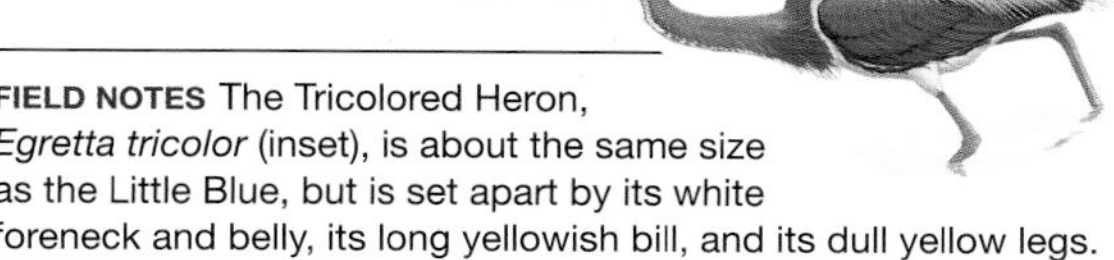

FIELD NOTES The Tricolored Heron, *Egretta tricolor* (inset), is about the same size as the Little Blue, but is set apart by its white foreneck and belly, its long yellowish bill, and its dull yellow legs. It is a year-round resident of the Carolinas' coastal salt marshes.

Year-round | Adult

GREEN HERON

Butorides virescens L 18" (46 cm) W 26" (66 cm)

FIELD MARKS

Small, chunky heron with blue-green back and crown, sometimes raised to form shaggy crest

Back and sides of neck deep chestnut, throat white

Short yellow to orange legs

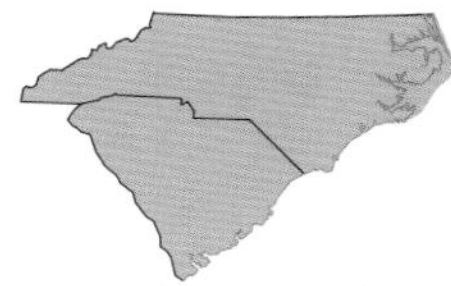

Behavior

Usually a solitary hunter, a Green Heron that lands near one of its kind is likely to be attacked. Look for the bird standing motionless in or near water, waiting for a fish to come close enough for a swift attack. The Green Heron spends most of its day in the shade, sometimes perched in trees or shrubs. When alarmed, it may make a show by flicking its tail, raising its crest, and elongating its neck, revealing streaked throat plumage. Its common cry of *kyowk* may be heard as it flies away.

Habitat

Found in a variety of wetland habitats but prefers streams, ponds, and marshes with woodland cover.

Local Sites

Look for this bird at water's edge, waiting motionless for prey to come near, in open areas of ACE Basin, Alligator River, and Mattamuskeet National Widlife Refuges, or at similar sites farther inland.

FIELD NOTES An innovative hunter, the Green Heron will sometimes, though rarely, stand at the edge of shallow water and toss twigs, insects, even earthworms into the water as lures to attract unsuspecting minnows into its striking range. This is one of the few instances of tool use in the bird world.

Breeding | Adult

BLACK-CROWNED NIGHT-HERON

Nycticorax nycticorax L 25" (64 cm) W 44" (112 cm)

FIELD MARKS

Black crown and back

Two to three white hindneck plumes, longest when breeding

White underparts and face; gray wings, tail, and sides of neck

Immature streaked brown

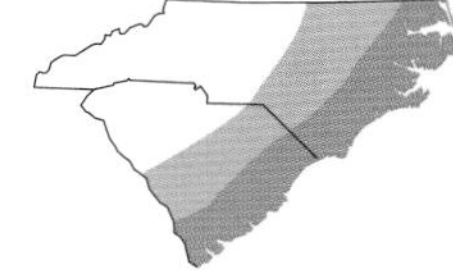

Behavior

Primarily a nocturnal feeder. Even when feeding during the day, remains in the shadows, almost motionless, waiting for prey to come within range. Forages for fish, frogs, rodents, reptiles, mollusks, eggs, and nestlings. Black-crowneds, consumers of fairly large prey, are susceptible to accumulating contaminants; their population status is an indicator of environmental quality. Call heard in flight is a gutteral *quok.*

Habitat

This heron has adapted to a wide range of habitats, including salt marshes, brackish and freshwater wetlands, and lakeshores that provide cover and forage. Nests in colonies high up in trees.

Local Sites

Scan the trees at any number of coastal spots for these nocturnal feeders roosting during the day with their bills tucked into their neck feathers.

FIELD NOTES The adult Yellow-crowned Night-Heron, *Nyctanassa violacea* (inset), is also a nocturnal feeder adorned with long, white neck plumes. A head patterned in black and white and a largely gray body distinguish the Yellow-crowned from its cousin.

Year-round | Adult

WHITE IBIS

Eudocimus albus L 25" (64 cm) W 38" (97 cm

FIELD MARKS

White plumage and red facial skin

Long, reddish, decurved bill; reddish legs and feet

Black tips of primary flight feathers show in flight

Immatures brown above

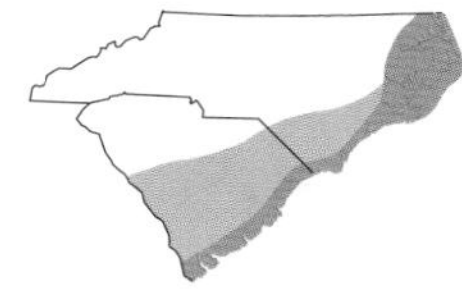

Behavior

Feeds in small groups, wading through shallow water or marshland, thrusting its bill into soil to probe for prey. Also sieves water for food with its bill. During courtship, a mating pair rub their heads together, offer grass and sticks to each other, and engage in mutual preening. Gathers in dense breeding colonies in trees or shrubs during spring and summer. Listen for the male's *hunk-hunk-hunk-hunk* call.

Habitat

Abundant in coastal salt marshes and swamps. Also found in coastal lagoons and croplands. Builds nests in trees or bushes, often on islands offering protection against predation.

Local Sites

Look for White Ibises in marshes and on mudflats along the length of the Carolinas' coastline. Huntington Beach State Park and Pea Island National Wildlife Refuge are two reliable spots.

FIELD NOTES The Glossy Ibis, *Plegadis falcinellus*, (inset) shares the same coastal habitat as the White Ibis; both are currently expanding north up the Atlantic seaboard. The Glossy Ibis looks all black from a distance, but its chestnut plumage is glossed with green or purple.

Year-round | Adult

TURKEY VULTURE

Cathartes aura L 27" (69 cm) W 69" (175 cm)

FIELD MARKS

In flight, two-toned underwings contrast and long tail extends beyond feet

Brownish black feathers on body; silver-gray flight feathers

Unfeathered red head; ivory bill; pale legs

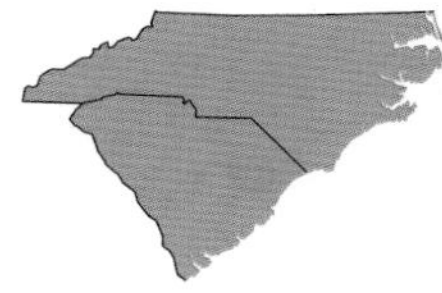

Behavior

An adept flier, the Turkey Vulture soars high above the ground in search of carrion and refuse. Rocks from side to side in flight, seldom flapping its wings, which are held upward in a shallow V, allowing it to gain lift from conditions that would deter many other raptors. Well developed sense of smell allows the Turkey Vulture to locate carrion concealed in forest settings. Feeds heavily when food is available but can go days without if necessary. Generally silent.

Habitat

Hunts in open country, woodlands, farms, even in urban dumps and landfills. Often seen over highways, searching for roadkill. Nests solitarily in abandoned buildings or hollow logs and trees.

Local Sites

Turkey Vultures are abundant year-round residents in wooded or open areas across the Carolinas.

FIELD NOTES The less common Black Vulture, *Coragyps atratus* (inset), is not as efficient at finding a meal, but just as aggressive. It will sometimes follow a Turkey Vulture to its find and claim it as its own. Unfeathered heads and hooked bills aid both species in consuming carrion.

Year-round | Adult male

OSPREY

Pandion haliaetus L 22-25" (56-64 cm) W 58-72" (147-183 cm)

FIELD MARKS

Dark brown above, white below; female has darker neck streaks

White head, dark eye stripe

Slightly arched in flight, wings appear bent back or "crooked"

Pale plumage fringing in juvenile

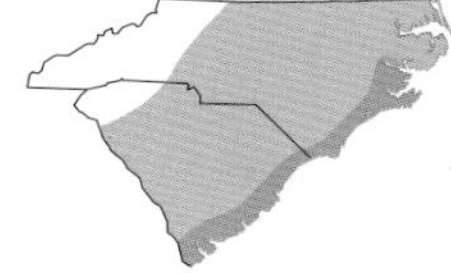

Behavior

Hunts by soaring, hovering, then diving down and plunging feet-first into water, snatching its prey with long, lethal talons. Feeds exclusively on fish. Call a series of clear, resonant, whistled *kyew*s. During breeding season, a male Osprey may call to draw a female's attention to a prized fish hooked in his talons.

Habitat

Nests near bodies of fresh or saltwater. Its bulky nests are built atop dead trees or on specialized man-made platforms. Uncommon inland, yet found on all continents except Antarctica.

Local Sites

Ospreys can be found throughout most of the Carolinas, wherever fish are abundant and trees or platforms provide suitable nesting locations. Look for them on the coast or at large inland lakes.

FIELD NOTES Also primarily a fish eater, the Bald Eagle, *Haliaeetus leucocephalus* (inset), inhabits wetland habitats rich in prey. A majestic soarer, it rarely needs to flap its long wings. Look for its stark white head extending beyond its dark brown body in flight. It can be seen year-round in the skies above the Carolinas' coastal plain.

Year-round | Adult

MISSISSIPPI KITE

Ictinia mississippiensis L 14½" (37 cm) W 35" (89 cm)

FIELD MARKS

Long, pointed wings; first primary distinctly shorter than others

Dark gray above, paler below and on head; black tail

Male's head paler than female's

Juvenile streaked brown overall

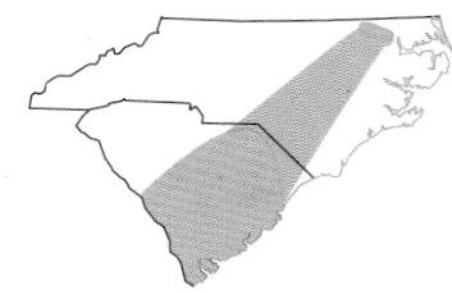

Behavior

A smooth, swift flier, the Mississippi Kite pursues, captures, and eats its prey, mostly cicadas, dragonflies, and other insects, on the wing. It can remain in flight for hours on end. A gregarious bird, it will hunt in groups, often in proximity of livestock. Not territorial even in breeding season, several may perch in trees together. Mates arrive in spring from the neotropics already paired and nest in loose colonies. Though usually silent, sometimes emits a high, whistled, downslurred *pe-teew.*

Habitat

Found in woodlands, swamps, or over open areas such as fields or golf courses. Makes nest of green leaves and Spanish moss high up in tall trees.

Local Sites

In South Carolina, Mississippi Kites can be seen winging rapidly over Francis Marion National Forest, Francis Beidler Forest, or Congaree National Park. In North Carolina, scan the skies around Roanoke Rapids.

FIELD NOTES The Mississippi Kite, like other kites, lacks the bony ridge over its eyes, lending it a seemingly more benign countenance than most other hawks and eagles.

Juvenile

COOPER'S HAWK

Accipiter cooperii L 14-20" (36-51 cm) W 29-37" (74-94 cm)

FIELD MARKS

Blue-gray upperparts; reddish bars across breast, belly

Dark gray cap; bright red eyes

Long, rounded, barred tail with white terminal band

Juvenile brown with yellow eyes

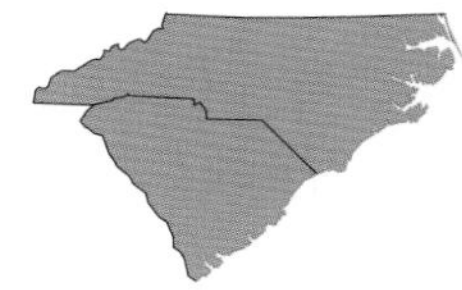

Behavior

Scans for prey from a perch, then attacks with a sudden burst of speed. Also scans for prey while soaring. Flies fast and close to the ground, using brush to conceal its rapid attack. Typically feeds on birds, rabbits, rodents, reptiles, and insects. Known to hold prey underwater to drown it. Uses a *kek-kek-kek* call at nest site.

Habitat

Prefers broken, especially deciduous, woodlands and streamside groves. Has adapted to fragmented woodlands created by urban and suburban development. Often found in larger trees in urban woods and parks.

Local Sites

National Forests throughout the Carolinas provide hunting grounds for Cooper's Hawks.

FIELD NOTES Distinguishing a Cooper's from a Sharp-shinned Hawk, *Accipiter striatus* (inset: juvenile, left; adult, right), is one of birding's more difficult identifications. Both species are largely brown as juveniles; blue-gray above, barred rufous below as adults. The Sharp-shinned is slightly smaller, has a more squared-off tail, and its neck does not extend as far from its body in flight.

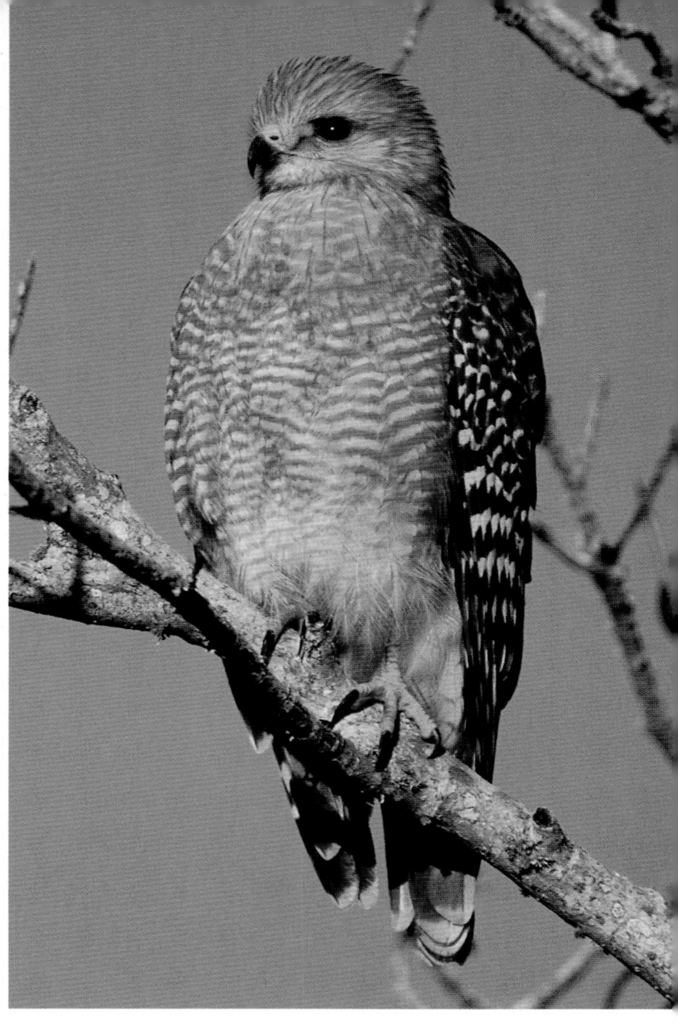

Year-round | Adult

RED-SHOULDERED HAWK

Buteo lineatus L 15-19" (38-48 cm) W 37-42" (94-107 cm)

FIELD MARKS

Adult has reddish shoulders and wing linings; pale spotting above

Breast barred reddish; head has a grayish cast

In flight, shows black tail with white bands and a pale crescent at base of primaries

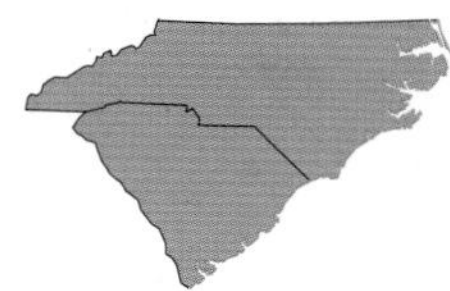

Behavior

The Red-shouldered Hawk flies with several wing beats, followed by a glide on flattened wings. Look for it during fall migration, saving its energy by soaring on rising currents of warm air, called thermals. Hunts from low perches for snakes, amphibians, small mammals, and an occasional small bird. Call is an evenly spaced series of clear, high *kee-ah* or *kah* notes.

Habitat

Prefers woodlands, especially moist, mixed woods near water and swamps. Nests close to tree trunks, 10 to 200 feet up. Returns to the same territory for years, sometimes passing nests along to succeeding generations.

Local Sites

Red-shouldered Hawks are most common in the Carolinas around the wooded wetlands of sites such as ACE Basin and Alligator River National Wildlife Refuges.

FIELD NOTES The Broad-winged Hawk, *Buteo platypterus* (inset), has wider bands on its tail and more white on its underwings than the Red-shouldered. It migrates through the Appalachian portion of the Carolinas around September, sometimes in flocks of thousands.

Year-round | Adult

RED-TAILED HAWK

Buteo jamaicensis L 22" (56 cm) W 50" (127 cm)

FIELD MARKS

Brown above; red tail on adults

Whitish belly with broad band of dark streaking

Dark bar on leading edge of underwing

Immature has brown, banded tail

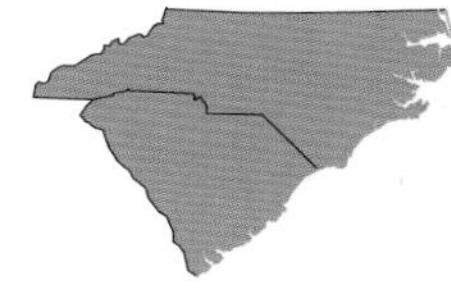

Behavior

Watch the Red-tailed Hawk circling above, searching for rodents, sometimes even kiting, or hanging motionless on the wind. Uses thermals to gain lift and limit its energy expenditure while soaring. Perches for long intervals on telephone poles and other manmade structures, often in urban areas. Listen for its distinctive call, a harsh, descending *keeeeeer.*

Habitat

Seen in more habitats than any other North American buteo, from woods with nearby open lands to plains and prairies. Scan along habitat edges, where field meets forest or wetlands meet woodlands, favored because of the variety of prey found there.

Local Sites

Red-taileds are one of the most common and easily seen hawks of North America. Widespread year-round, they perch near forest edges in wooded areas throughout the Carolinas.

FIELD NOTES While perched, Red-taileds are easy to spot, but when migrating, the hawks soar at altitudes up to 5,000 feet, appearing as nothing more than specks in the sky.

Year-round | Adult male

AMERICAN KESTREL

Falco sparverius L 10½" (27 cm) W 23" (58 cm)

FIELD MARKS

Barred russet back and tail

Two black stripes on white face

Male has blue-gray wing coverts; pale spotted underparts

Female has russet wing coverts; pale streaked underparts

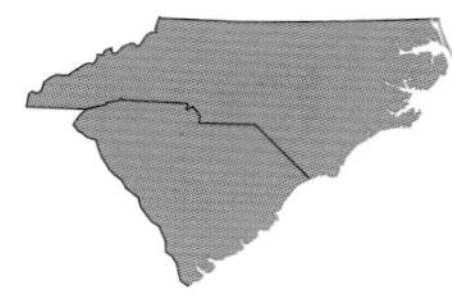

Behavior

Smallest of North American falcons, feeds on insects, reptiles, mice and other small mammals. Hovers over prey by coordinating its flight speed with the wind speed, then plunges down for the kill. Will also feed on small birds, especially in winter. Regularly seen perched on fences and telephone lines, bobbing its tail with frequency. Has clear, shrill call of *killy-killy-killy.*

Habitat

Found in open country and in cities, often mousing along highway medians or sweeping down shorelines. Nests in tree holes or barns using little nesting material. For not fully understood reasons, a major decline in the kestrel's eastern population has occurred recently.

Local Sites

Widespread year-round throughout the Carolinas. In fall, look for migrating kestrels in abundance from lookouts in Smoky Mountains National Park.

FIELD NOTES The larger Peregrine Falcon, *Falco peregrinus* (inset), migrating south from the Arctic in fall, is distinguished by its "helmet," the black on its crown and nape, which contrasts sharply with its pale neck. Look as well for the largely brown juvenile Peregrine (inset, right).

Year-round | Adult

CLAPPER RAIL

Rallus Longirostris L 14½" (37 cm)

FIELD MARKS

Grayish edges on brown-centered back feathers; olive wing coverts

Gray-brown flanks with white bars

Short tail; broad wings

Long, thin, slightly decurved bill

Grayish cheeks

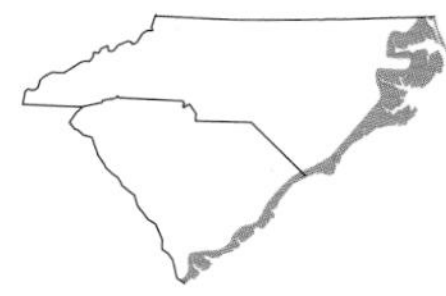

Behavior

This secretive bird usually remains concealed in marsh vegetation. Uses long, thin bill to probe into crevices and holes, such as those of fiddler crabs, worms, and other crustaceans, located under the surface of shallow water. Bobs its head and flicks its tail as it walks. Its distinctive call is an accelerating, then slowing, crescendo of ten or more *kek kek kek* notes, uttered year-round.

Habitat

Common in coastal salt marshes. Nests are deeply concealed and constructed of marsh vegetation.

Local Sites

Exclusively coastal, Clapper Rails inhabit salt marshes along the Carolinas' shoreline from Pinckney Island National Wildlife Refuge to Mackay Island National Wildlife Refuge. Scan marsh edges or along irrigation canals for at least a glimpse of these secretive birds.

FIELD NOTES Even where they are abundant, Clapper Rails can be extremely difficult to see. They are quite vocal, though. Listen for the domino effect of their distinctive calls especially around dawn and dusk as one call elicits another nearby.

Year-round | Adult

AMERICAN COOT

Fulica americana L 15½" (39 cm)

FIELD MARKS

Blackish head; slate gray body

Small, reddish brown forehead shield; reddish eyes on adult

Whitish bill with dark band at tip; greenish legs with lobed toes

Juvenile paler with darker bill

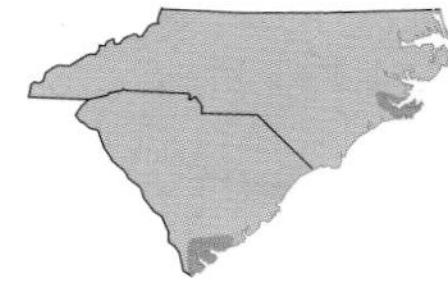

Behavior

The distinctive toes of the American Coot are flexible and lobed, permitting it to swim well in open water and even to dive in pursuit of aquatic vegetation and invertebrates. Lobed toes also enable the coot to run on water, flapping its wings rapidly in order to gain the momentum it needs to take flight. Forages in large flocks, especially during the winter. Has a wide vocabulary of grunts, quacks, and chatter.

Habitat

Nests in freshwater marshes or near lakes and ponds. Winters in both fresh and saltwater. The coot has also adapted to human-altered habitats, including sewage lagoons for foraging and suburban lawns for roosting.

Local Sites

Primarily winter visitors to the Carolinas, coots can be found in fairly sizable flocks at waterfowl stopovers such as Santee Coastal Reserve and Pea Island National Wildlife Refuge.

FIELD NOTES The slightly smaller Common Moorhen, *Gallinula chloropus* (inset), inhabits many of the same freshwater wetlands as the coot. It has a bright red forehead shield which extends onto a red bill tipped with yellow. The white line down its side is another good field mark.

Breeding | Adult

BLACK-BELLIED PLOVER

Pluvialis squatarola L 11½" (29 cm) W 45"

FIELD MARKS

Roundish head and body; large eyes; short black bill; dark legs

Mottled gray; white underparts in winter and juveniles

Breeding male has frosted cap; black and white spots on back and wings; black face and breast

Behavior

Hunts in small, loose groups for invertebrates such as mollusks, worms, shrimp, insects, and small crabs, along with eggs and sometimes berries. Locates prey by sight, runs across the ground, stops, then runs off again. In this respect, a plover has a similar hunting style to that of a thrush, such as an American Robin. Long, pointed wings enable swift flight. Listen for the Black-bellied Plover's drawn-out three-note whistle, *pee-oo-ee*, the second note lower in pitch.

Habitat

This shorebird prefers sandy beaches, mudflats, and salt marshes. Rarely found in interior regions. Breeds on the Arctic tundra.

Local Sites

Black-bellied Plovers can be found in the Carolinas primarily in their drab winter garb between August and April in sandy coastal areas such as Cape Hatteras National Seashore.

FIELD NOTES During spring migration, look for the Black-bellied's characteristic breeding plumage (opposite). During winter though, the Black-bellied sheds its contrasting black-and-white feathers and dons a drabber gray plumage (inset) to blend into its sandy Carolina environs.

Juvenile

SEMIPALMATED PLOVER

Charadrius semipalmatus L 7¼" (18 cm)

FIELD MARKS

Dark brown above, white below

Single breast band is gray-brown in winter, black during breeding

Short white supercilium

Juvenile has pale-fringed upperparts and darker legs

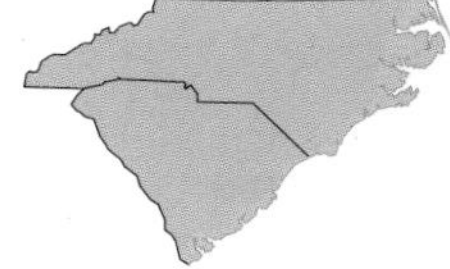

Behavior

Locates prey with its large eyes, then runs on the sand, stopping to probe for mollusks, worms, crustaceans, and buried eggs. Flocks often congregate at sundown, roosting communally with their heads tucked into their feathers. Distinctive call is a whistled, upslurred *chu-weet.* Song is a series of the same.

Habitat

Common on beaches, lakeshores, and tidal flats. Winters on coastlines, but seen throughout the continent during migration. Breeds in the Arctic.

Local Sites

Look for Semipalmated Sandpipers in winter on sandy beaches along the length of the Carolinas' coastline. Huntington Beach State Park is one good spot.

FIELD NOTES The endangered Piping Plover, *Charadrius melodus* (inset), which breeds locally on sandy beaches in Albemarle and Pamlico Sounds in North Carolina, is the same size as the Semipalmated and has in common with it a dark breast band and a black-tipped orange bill. The Piping's back is paler than the Semipalmated's, however, and its breast band is often incomplete.

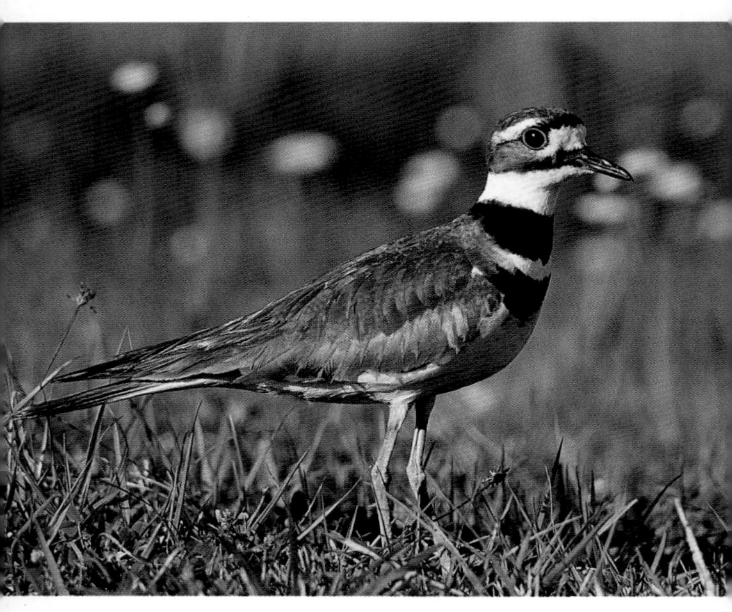

Year-round | Adult

KILLDEER

Charadrius vociferus L 10½" (27 cm)

FIELD MARKS

Gray-brown above; white neck and belly; two black breast bands

Black stripe on forehead and one extending back from black bill

Red-orange rump visible in flight

Red orbital ring

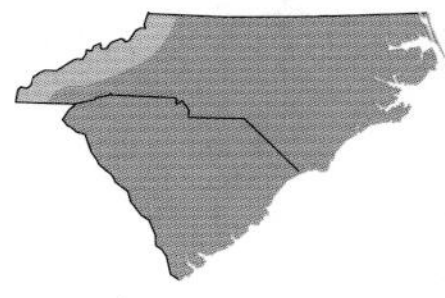

Behavior

Often seen running, then stopping on a dime with an inquisitive look, then suddenly jabbing at the ground with its bill. Feeds mainly on insects that live in short vegetation. May gather in loose flocks. The Killdeer's loud, piercing, eponymous call of *kill-dee* or its rising *dee-dee-dee* is often the signal for identifying these birds before sighting them. Listen also for a long, trilled *trrrrrrr* during courtship displays or when a nest is threatened by a predator.

Habitat

Although a type of plover—one of the shorebirds—the Killdeer prefers inland grassy regions, but also may be found on shores. Builds its nest on open ground.

Local Sites

Killdeers can be found in open areas along the Carolinas' coast or farther inland at sites such as Super Sod Farms near Orangeburg, South Carolina.

FIELD NOTES If its nest is threatened by an intruder, the Killdeer is known to feign a broken wing, limping to one side, dragging its wing, and spreading its tail in an attempt to lure the threat away from its young. Once the predator is far enough away from the nest, the "instantly healed" Killdeer takes flight.

Year-round | Adult

AMERICAN OYSTERCATCHER

Haematopus palliatus L 18½" (47 cm)

FIELD MARKS

Large, red-orange bill; pink legs

Black head and neck; dark brown back and tail

White underparts and wing stripe

Juvenile is scaly-looking above, with dark tip on bill

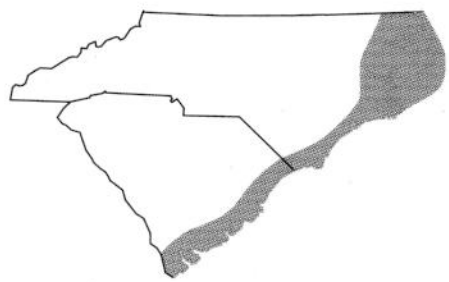

Behavior

Feeds in shallow water alone or in a flock. It uses its chisel-shaped bill to crack an opening in the shells of clams, oysters, and mussels; it then severs the shellfish's constrictor muscle and pries the shell open. Also probes sand and mud for worms and crabs. Courtship consists of calls coupled with ritualized flights of shallow, rapid wing beats and displays of side-by-side running or rotating in place. Calls are vocal and variable, including a piercing, repeated whistle; a loud, piping *queep*; and a single loud whistle.

Habitat

Coastal beaches, mudflats, and rocky outcroppings. Nests in a bowl-shaped depression in sand or grass, or on gravel and shells piled above the tide line.

Local Sites

Oystercatchers keep to the coast year-round at sites such as Cape Romain National Wildlife Refuge and Fort Fisher State Recreation Area, where a three-mile hike along a narrow spit of land can bring you close to a nesting pair.

FIELD NOTES American Oystercatchers are quite wary of humans and generally do not allow close approach. Keep an ear out though for their loud calls which are as distinctive as their bills.

Year-round | Adult male

BLACK-NECKED STILT

Himantopus mexicanus L 14" (36 cm)

FIELD MARKS

Males dark black from head, down back, to tail; female and juveniles tinged dark brown

White below and around eyes

Glossy black, needle-thin bill

Very long red or pink legs

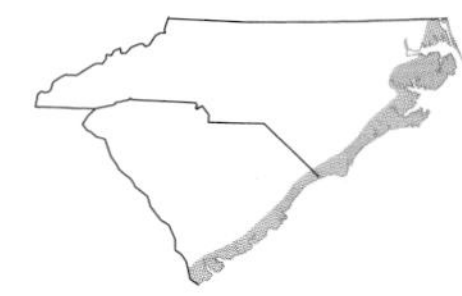

Behavior

Tall and elegant, the Black-necked Stilt feeds quietly in small groups or by itself. Exceptionally long legs allow it to forage in deeper water than most shorebirds. As it strides gracefully through the water, it picks small organisms from the surface. When disturbed, stilts are very noisy, their sharp calls, *pleek-pleek-pleek*, piercing the air as they take flight.

Habitat

Adaptable to a wide variety of wet habitats, the stilt is partial to freshwater and is locally common in shallow, marshy, or muddy ponds. Nests on the ground, concealed in grass.

Local Sites

Favored nesting locales of Black-necked Stilts in the Carolinas include Santee Coastal Reserve, as well as ACE Basin and Pea Island National Wildlife Refuges.

FIELD NOTES The American Avocet, *Recurvirostra americana* (inset), is the only other North American member of the family *Recurvirostridae*. The Avocet's bill is long, thin, black, and upcurved. Its gray head and neck in winter and its white scapulars set the Avocet apart from its cousin.

Nonbreeding | Adult

GREATER YELLOWLEGS

Tringa melanoleuca L 14" (36 cm)

FIELD MARKS

Long, dark, slightly upturned bill; long, bright yellow-orange legs

Head and neck streaked gray-brown; white-speckled, gray-brown back

White underparts slightly barred gray-brown on flanks

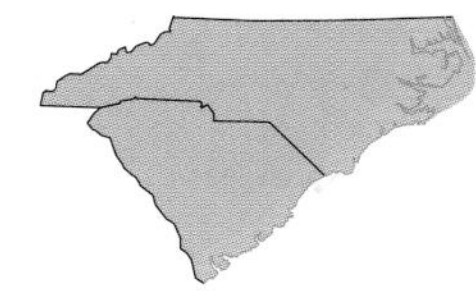

Behavior

A forager of snails, crabs, and shrimp; also skims surface of water for insects and larvae. Sprints short distances in pursuit of small fish. Usually seen alone or in small groups, this wary bird sounds an alarm when a hawk or falcon approaches. Call is distinctive series of three or more loud, repeated, descending *tew-tew-tew* sounds, heard most often in flight.

Habitat

In winter, frequents a full range of wetlands, including marshes, ponds, lakes, rivers, and reservoirs. Breeds across the Canadian boreal zone.

Local Sites

Primarily coastal birds in the Carolinas, Greater Yellowlegs can be found in winter along with their smaller cousins, the Lesser Yellowlegs, in sandy environs such as those at Huntington Beach State Park and Cape Lookout National Seashore.

FIELD NOTES The Lesser Yellowlegs, *Tringa flavipes* (inset), shares much of the Greater's winter habitat. Distinguished by its shorter, straighter bill—about the length of its head—it is smaller in stature and less wary in behavior. The Lesser's call is higher and shorter too, consisting of one or two *tew* notes.

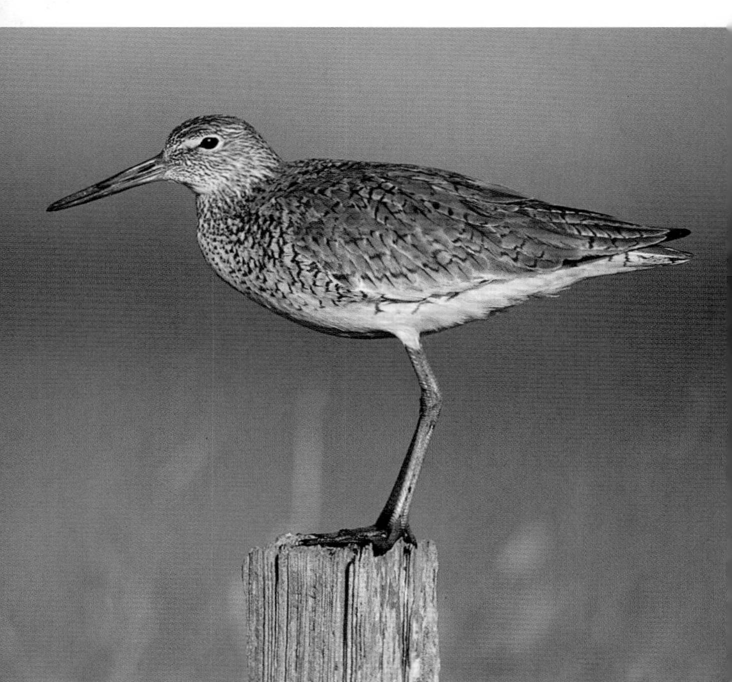

Breeding | Adult

WILLET

Catoptrophorus semipalmatus L 15" (38 cm)

FIELD MARKS

Large and plump; long gray legs

Breeding adult is heavily mottled brownish gray above; white belly

Winter plumage pale gray above

In flight, shows black-and-white wing pattern

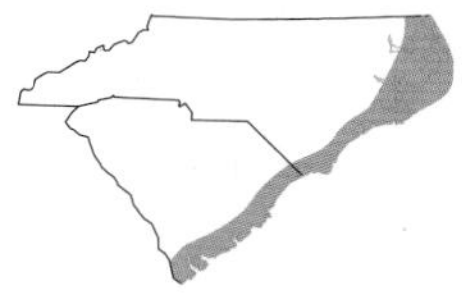

Behavior

The Willet, like other shorebirds, wades in search of prey, probing through mud with its long bill. Feeds primarily on aquatic insects and their larvae. During courtship displays, the Willet will show its black-and-white underwing bands, one of its most identifiable field marks. Its breeding call of *pill-o-will-willet* is the origin of its name; it may also be heard giving a *kip-kip-kip* alarm call.

Habitat

Common on beaches and coastal salt marshes. Nests on sand in grassy vegetation.

Local Sites

Coastally ubiquitous, Willets can be found at any number of sites along the Carolinas' shoreline. Pea Island and Cape Romain National Wildlife Refuges are two good spots.

FIELD NOTES The Ruddy Turnstone, *Arenaria interpres* (inset), is another shorebird characterized in flight by a striking black-and-white wing pattern. It is considerably smaller than the Willet, and has a black bib on its breast.

Nonbreeding | Adult

SPOTTED SANDPIPER

Actitis macularia L 7½" (19 cm)

FIELD MARKS

Olive-brown upperparts, barred during breeding season

White underparts, spotted brown while breeding

Short, straight orange bill tipped in black

Short white wing stripe in flight

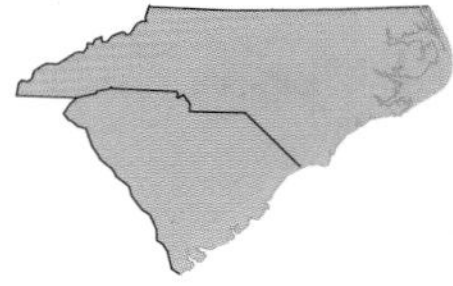

Behavior

Feeds on insects, crustaceans, and other invertebrates by plucking them from the water's surface or snatching them from the air. Walks with a constant teetering motion. Generally stands with tail up and head down. Flies with stiff, rapid, fluttering wing beats. Calls include a shrill *peet-weet* and a series of *weet* notes, given in flight.

Habitat

One of the most common and widespread sandpipers in North America during breeding season, preferring sheltered ponds, lakes, streams, or marshes. Winters in the Carolinas on rocky shorelines.

Local Sites

Look for the spotted underparts of these sandpipers only in portions of the Appalachians between April and August. In winter, you can find them along the coast of South Carolina.

FIELD NOTES In the Carolinas, the Spotted Sandpiper breeds only in a small portion of the Appalachians. Breeding plumage is characterized by dark brown spots on white underparts. The larger female is the first to establish territory and to defend it during breeding season. She may also mate with several males in a single season while the males tend to the eggs and young.

Molting | Adult

SANDERLING

Calidris alba L 8" (20 cm)

FIELD MARKS

Winter adult pale gray above, white below

Bill and legs black

Prominent white wing stripe and black leading edge show in flight

Juveniles black-and-white above

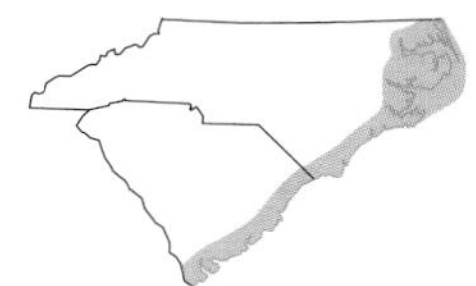

Behavior

Feeds on sandy beaches, chasing retreating waves in order to snatch up newly exposed crustaceans and mollusks, then darting to avoid oncoming surf. Like many shorebirds, may be seen standing for a long time on one leg. Flies swiftly, aided by ample wing length and sharp, pointed wings. Flocks wheel and turn together in the air. Call is a sharp *kip*, often emitted in a series.

Habitat

Winters on sandy beaches of the United States and throughout most of the Southern Hemisphere. Migrates sometimes as many as 8,000 miles from breeding grounds in remote Arctic and subarctic.

Local Sites

A common sight on almost any sandy beach of the Carolinas in winter. Look for a Sanderling beginning to acquire a rusty wash on its head and back before departing for breeding grounds in early May.

FIELD NOTES The Dunlin, *Calidris alpina* (inset), is another small, pale winter inhabitant of the Carolinas' sandy shorelines. It is slightly darker above and has a diffuse, dark gray breast band. Its bill is also longer and slightly decurved toward the tip.

Nonbreeding | Adult

LEAST SANDPIPER

Calidris minutilla L 6" (15 cm)

FIELD MARKS

Short, thin, slightly decurved bill

Gray-brown upperparts

Streaked gray-brown breast band

White belly and undertail coverts

Yellowish to greenish legs

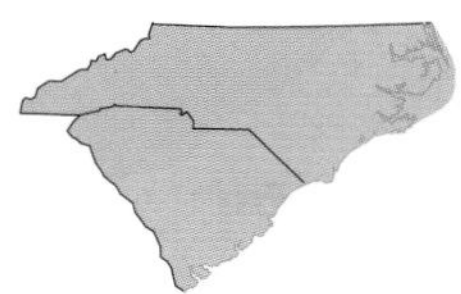

Behavior

Forages for food with its stout, spiky bill. Feeds on worms, insects, mollusks, small crabs, and fish, in muddy, sandy, or shallow water. Not wary of humans, it will investigate picnic sites on the beach. If flushed, flies off rapidly in a zigzag flight pattern. The Least Sandpiper's call is a high *kreee.*

Habitat

Common in coastal tidal regions and wetlands with exposed mud or sand. Flocks of up to 50 birds can appear on exposed mudflats both on the coast and inland. Breeds in Arctic regions.

Local Sites

Common along the entire length of the shoreline and considerably inland as well, look for Least Sandpipers primarily in mudflats and marshes on the bay side of the Carolinas' barrier islands.

FIELD NOTES The most diminutive of shorebirds collectively known as "peeps," the Least Sandpiper's yellow-green legs set it apart from the slightly larger Western Sandpiper, *Calidris mauri*, which has black legs. The Least's bill is also slightly shorter and its breast band more pronounced. These two peeps' winter range in the Carolinas overlaps only near the coast.

Nonbreeding | Adult

SHORT-BILLED DOWITCHER

Limnodromus griseus L 11" (28 cm)

FIELD MARKS

In winter, brownish gray above, white below with gray breast

Long dark bill

Distinct pale eyebrow

Juvenile has rufous edges on back feathers and buffy breast

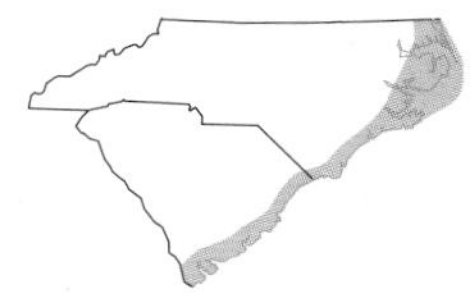

Behavior

Probes mud for insects with rapid up-down stitching motion of bill, often submerging head in water. Roosts in fairly large flocks and interacts often with other species, including its close relative, the Long-billed Dowitcher. The Short-billed's song is a rapid *di-di-da-doo*, and its alarm call is a mellow *tu-tu-tu,* repeated in a series.

Habitat

Prefers open marshes, mudflats, and shallow ponds along the coastline. Breeds on subarctic tundra.

Local Sites

Short-billed Dowitchers can be found in winter along with their closely related cousins, the Long-billed Dowitchers, in mudflats and marshes along the length of the Carolinas' immediate coastline.

FIELD NOTES The closely related Long-billed Dowitcher, *Limnodromus scolopaceus* (inset), is only slightly larger and only the female's bill is longer than the Short-billed's. The Long-billed is more vocal than its cousin, uttering a sharp high-pitched *keek* call in flight. Both species have a V-shaped white patch extending up the back from the tail.

Year-round | Adult

WILSON'S SNIPE

Gallinago gallinago L 10¼" (26 cm)

FIELD MARKS

Stocky with very long bill and very short tail and pointed wings

Head and back boldly striped blackish brown and pale buff

Heavily barred flanks

Dark underwings, white belly

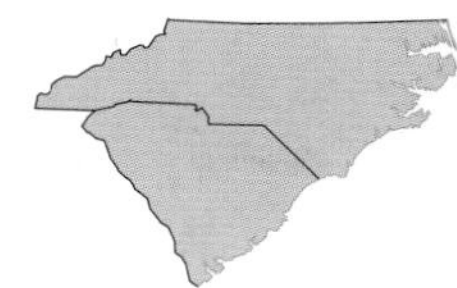

Behavior

This winter resident is often not seen until flushed, when it gives harsh *ski-ape* call and rapidly flies off in zigzag pattern. Feeds on insects, larvae, and earthworms by probing mud with its bill in a jerky fashion. Generally solitary, the snipe does not interact with other shorebirds. In swooping flight display, known as "winnowing," a quavering hoot-like sound is produced by air vibrating the two outermost tail feathers.

Habitat

Found in freshwater marshes and swamps and in any damp, muddy wetland where cover is afforded by vegetation. May frequent open areas as well.

Local Sites

Closely scan the ground around flooded fields on the Carolinas' coastal plain at sites such as Alligator River National Wildlife Refuge for this often overlooked bird.

FIELD NOTES Another stocky sandpiper to inhabit moist interior woodland is the American Woodcock, *Scolopax minor* (inset). As with the snipe, the woodcock is generally not seen until flushed when it flies off low to the ground, its rounded wings creating a loud twittering sound on takeoff.

Breeding | Adult

LAUGHING GULL

Larus atricilla L 16½" (42 cm) W 40" (102 cm)

FIELD MARKS

Breeding adult has black hood; white underparts; slate gray wings with black outer primaries

White crescent marks above and below eyes; drooping red bill

In winter, gray wash on head, nape, and neck; black bill

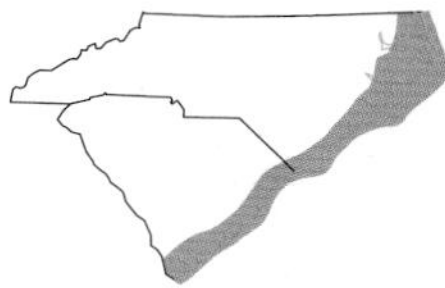

Behavior

Forages for crabs, insects, decayed fish, garbage, and anything else it can get, sometimes plunging its head underwater or harassing beachgoers for popcorn or french fries. In spring, large flocks can be observed feeding on deposits of horseshoe-crab eggs in wet sand. Name comes from characteristic call, *ha-ha-ha-ha*, given when feeding or courting.

Habitat

Common and conspicuous along coastal regions, especially sandy beaches. Nests of grass and aquatic plants are found in marshes or on sand.

Local Sites

The full black hood of the breeding Laughing Gull is hard to miss in summer in marshes and beaches along the length of the Carolinas' coast.

FIELD NOTES It takes three years for the Laughing Gull to attain full adult plumage. The juvenile is brown with a white throat and belly. By the first winter (inset), it still has brown wings, but its sides and back are gray. By the second winter it has lost all brown. Not until the third summer though does it develop a black hood, the sign of a full breeding adult.

Nonbreeding | Adult

RING-BILLED GULL

Larus delawarensis L 17½" (45 cm) W 48" (122 cm)

FIELD MARKS

Yellow bill with black subterminal ring; pale eye with dark orbital ring

Pale gray upperparts; white underparts; yellowish legs; black primaries show white spots

Head streaked brown in winter

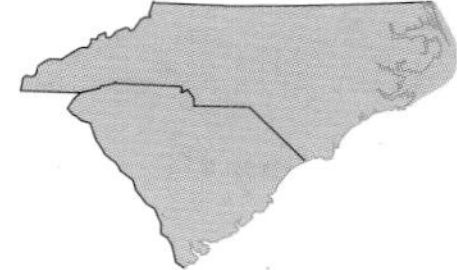

Behavior

This opportunistic feeder will scavenge for garbage, grains, dead fish, fruit, and marine invertebrates, often demanding scraps of food from beachgoers. A vocal gull, it calls, croaks, and cries incessantly, especially while feeding. Its call consists of a series of laughing croaks that begins with a short, gruff note and falls into a series of *kheeyaahhh* sounds. The Ring-billed takes three years to attain full adult plumage; the first winter Ring-billed has a pinkish bill with a dark tip.

Habitat

More common along the coast, but also a regular visitor to most inland bodies of water, especially reservoirs in urban areas.

Local Sites

Abundant in winter throughout coastal regions of the Carolinas, the Ring-billed Gull also frequents a multitude of parking lots, shopping centers, and garbage dumps inland.

FIELD NOTES The Ring-billed along with its partner in crime, the Herring Gull, are two of the most conspicuous gulls in the Carolinas. Adults are similar in plumage color and pattern, but the Herring Gull is noticeably larger.

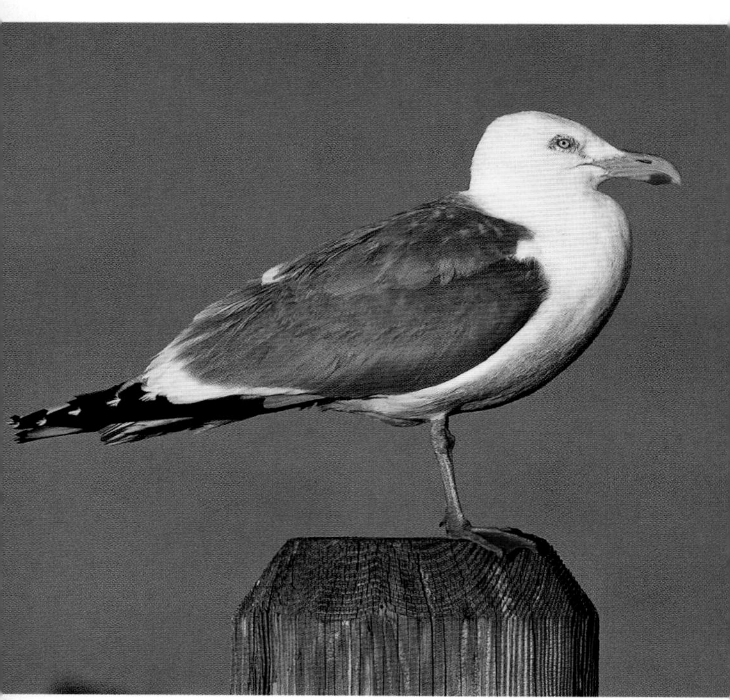

Breeding | Adult

HERRING GULL

Larus argentatus L 25" (64 cm) W 58" (147 cm)

FIELD MARKS

Yellow bill with red mark near tip of lower mandible

Pale gray mantle in adult

White head and neck streaked with brown in winter

Pinkish legs and feet

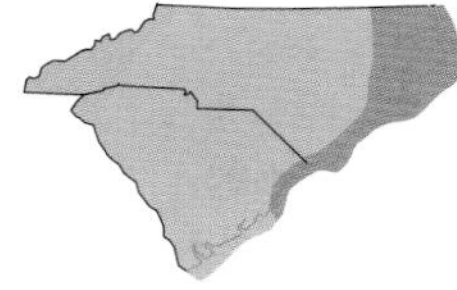

Behavior

Like other gulls, the Herring Gull forages on land and in sea for shellfish, dead fish, and marine invertebrates. Flocks congregate where food is abundant, such as at garbage dumps, near boardwalks, in parking lots, or around fishing boats. An aggressive forager, the Herring is known to steal lunches from other birds. Various calls include *cleew cleew*, *kyow*, and *kee-oo kee-oo*. Alarm call is a quick *kek kek kek*.

Habitat

Primarily a coastal bird, the Herring Gull is numerous along the coast, and less common but still widespread inland. Generally nests on the ground, but will move to trees or rooftops if pressed.

Local Sites

Found year-round along the Carolinas' coast south to Cape Romain. Herring Gulls move inland for winter, though not in great abundance.

FIELD NOTES An even larger and more aggressive forager, the Great Black-backed Gull, *Larus marinus* (inset), remains for the most part in coastal regions of the Carolinas. It too has a red spot near the tip of its lower mandible, but is easily set apart by its black mantle and upper wings.

Breeding | Adult

ROYAL TERN

Sterna maxima L 20" (51 cm) W 41" (104 cm)

FIELD MARKS

Full black cap acquired briefly, early in breeding season

White crown with black on nape for rest of year

White below, pale gray mantle

Orange-red bill; tail deeply forked

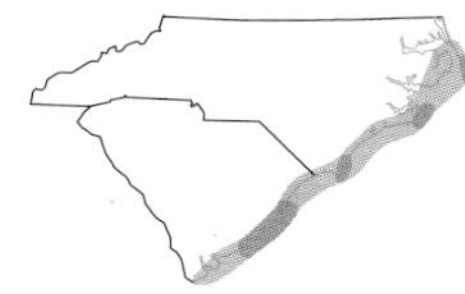

Behavior

Hovers, then plunge-dives 40 to 60 feet into water after prey of fish, shrimp, and crustaceans. Roosts along with other species of terns and gulls on sandbars, beaches, or mudflats. Small groups may cooperate in finding prey; once a school of fish is found, the entire group will soon congregate at that location. Calls in the Royal Tern's large vocabulary include a bleating *kee-rer* and a whistled *tourreee.* Juvenile emits a thin *see see see.*

Habitat

Prefers open salt water along coastlines, especially bays and inlets. Nests in dense, mixed colonies with other tern species on sandbars and small, sandy islands.

Local Sites

Winter residents along the Carolinas' coast north to Roanoke Island, Royals Terns tend to nest as far from humans as possible on the Carolinas' multiple capes.

FIELD NOTES The slightly larger Caspian Tern, *Sterna caspia* (inset), is not nearly as sociable as the Royal Tern and will eat the eggs and young of other tern species. Its bill is thicker and deeper red, the tips of its primaries are duskier, and its tail is not as deeply forked as the Royal's.

Molting | Adult

FORSTER'S TERN

Sterna forsteri L 14½" (37 cm)

FIELD MARKS

Pale gray above; white below

Full black cap on breeding adult; only around eye in fall and winter

Orange-red bill with dark tip while breeding; all dark in winter

Long, deeply forked gray tail

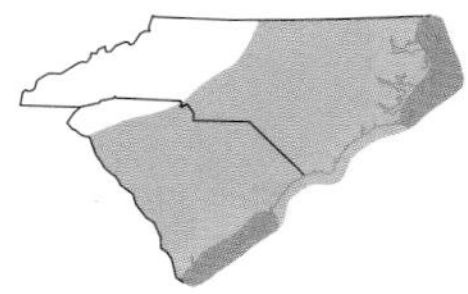

Behavior

When feeding, the Forster's flies back and forth over the water, then plunge-dives to capture small fish. May also forage on insects, grabbing them in the air or from the water's surface. Often feeds and flocks with other species of tern. Gives a one-note call, a hoarse, descending *kyarr*, while feeding over water or during breeding season. Also emits a piercing *kit-kit-kit* cry.

Habitat

Winters mainly along coastlines, but also inhabits inland marshes and lakes where abundant fish and insects may be found. Nests in loose colonies atop floating reeds, or in sand or mud.

Local Sites

Wintering the entirety of the coast and slightly inland, Forster's Terns nest on North Carolina's Outer Banks and on South Carolina's Sea Islands.

FIELD NOTES The endangered Least Tern, *Sterna antillarum* (inset), nests on sandy beaches and gravelly rooftops along the length of the Carolinas' coast. It is considerably smaller than the Forster's Tern; in fact it is the smallest tern to occur in North America. It has yellow bill and legs and a white forehead, and shows a black wedge on its outer primaries in flight.

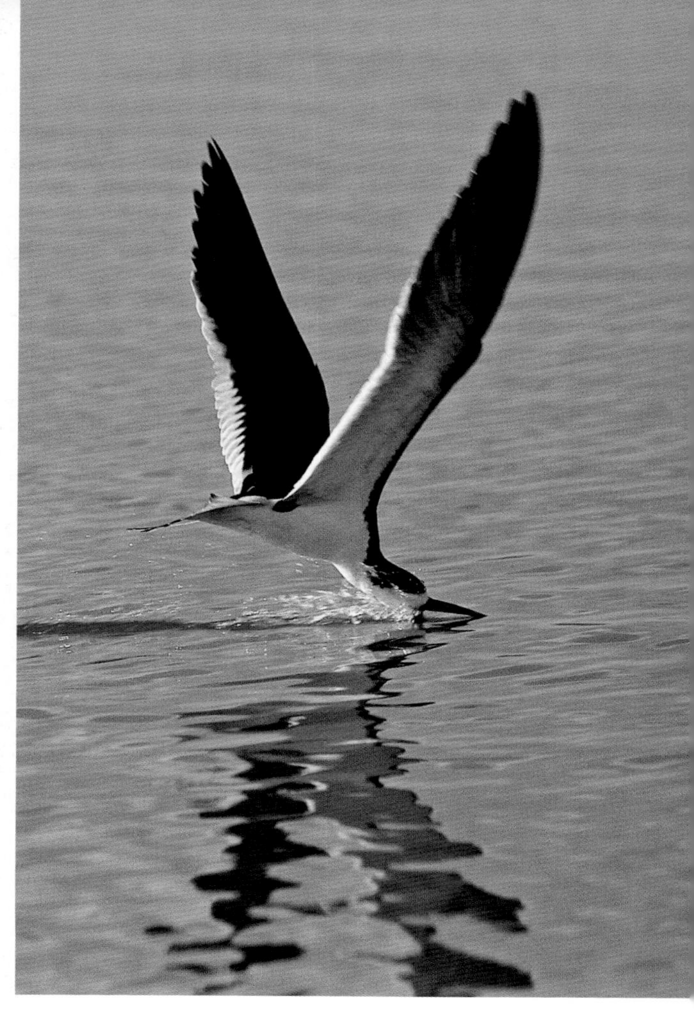

Breeding | Adult

BLACK SKIMMER

Rynchops niger L 18" (46 cm) W 44" (112 cm)

FIELD MARKS

Long, red, black-tipped bill

Black back and crown; white face and underparts; red legs

Winter adults show white collar

Female distinctly smaller

Juvenile mottled brown above

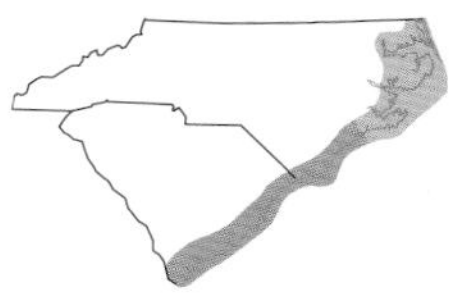

Behavior

Uses long, pointed wings to glide low over water while dropping its lower mandible to skim the surface for small fish. Once its bill touches a fish, the maxilla, or upper bill, snaps down to catch prey. Breeds in colonies on beaches, often sharing a site with tern species to take advantage of their aggressive defensive tactics. Makes a yelping bark in nesting colonies or in response to a threat. Pairs sometimes sing a *kow-kow* call together.

Habitat

Prefers sheltered bays, estuaries, coastal marshes, and sometimes inland lakes. Nests very locally in large colonies on barrier islands and salt marshes.

Local Sites

Black Skimmers can be seen year-round along the Carolinas' coast south from Onslow Bay and in summer in North Carolina's Outer Banks. An excellent spot to scan for them is from Moore's Landing at Cape Romain National Wildlife Refuge.

FIELD NOTES The Black Skimmer has a distinctive bill: As a feeding adaptation, the lower mandible is considerably longer than the upper. It also has an adaptive pupil, able to contract to a narrow, vertical slit. This capability is thought to protect the eye from bright sunlight glaring off the water's surface.

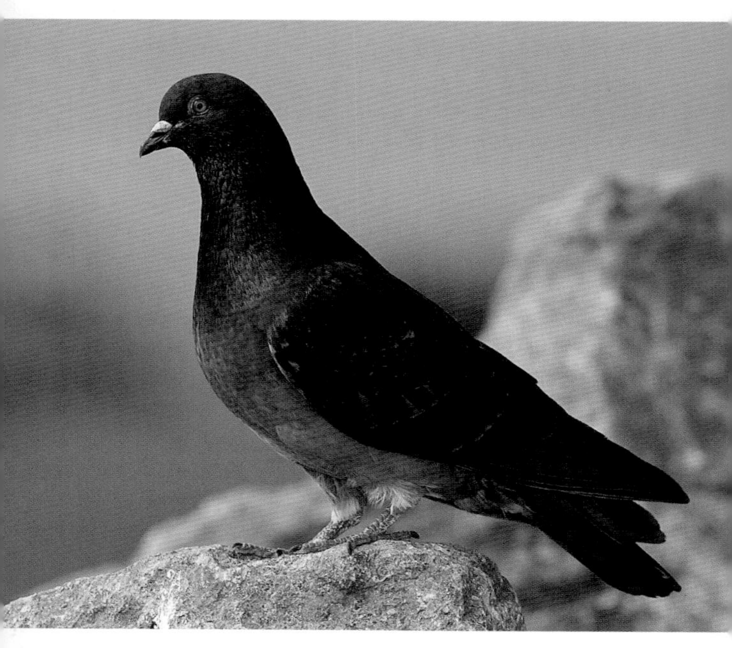

Year-round | Adult

ROCK PIGEON

Columba livia L 12½" (32 cm)

FIELD MARKS

Highly variable in its multicolored hues, with head and neck usually darker than back

White cere at base of dark bill, pink legs

Iridescent feathers on neck reflect green, bronze, and purple

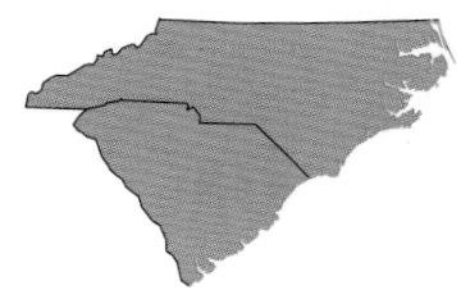

Behavior

Feeds during the day on grain, seeds, fruit, or refuse in cities and suburbs, parks, and fields; a frequent visitor to farms and backyard feeding stations as well. As it forages, the Rock Pigeon moves with a short-stepped, "pigeon-toed" gait while its head bobs back and forth. Courtship display consists of the male puffing out neck feathers, fanning his tail, and turning in circles while cooing; results in a pairing that could last for life. Characterized by soft *coo-cuk-cuk-cuk-cooo* call.

Habitat

Anywhere near human habitation. Nests and roosts primarily on high window ledges, on bridges, and in barns. Builds nest of stiff twigs, sticks, and leaves.

Local Sites

Introduced from Europe by settlers in the 1600s, the Rock Pigeon is now widespread and abundant throughout most developed regions of North America.

FIELD NOTES A highly variable species, the Rock Pigeon's colors range from rust red to all white to mosaic, due to centuries of selective breeding. Those resembling their wild ancestors have a dark head and neck, two black wing bars, and a white rump.

Year-round | Adult male

MOURNING DOVE

Zenaida macroura L 12" (31 cm)

FIELD MARKS

Gray-brown; black spots on upper wings; white tips on outer tail feathers show in flight

Trim-bodied; long pointed tail

Black spot on lower cheek; pinkish wash on neck in male

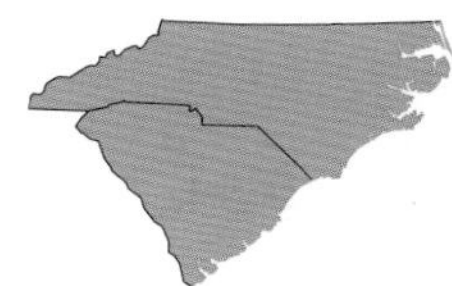

Behavior

Generally a ground feeder, the Mourning Dove forages for grains, seeds, grasses, and insects. Like other *Columbidae*, it is able to slurp up water without tipping back its head. Also able to produce "pigeon milk" in its crop lining, which it regurgitates to young during their first few days. Wings produce a fluttering whistle as the bird takes flight. Known for mournful call, *oowooo-woo-woo-woo*, given by males during breeding season.

Habitat

Widespread and abundant, the Mourning Dove is found in a variety of habitats, but prefers open areas, often choosing suburban sites for feeding and nesting.

Local Sites

Mourning Doves are abundant throughout the Carolinas, from wooded settings to farm fields to cities and towns.

FIELD NOTES An introduced species, the Eurasian Collared-Dove, *Streptopelia decaocto* (inset), has recently spread north up the Atlantic Coast to North Carolina. Its tail is more rounded than the Mourning's when perched, and its primaries are darker in flight. Look as well for its black collar trimmed in white.

Year-round | Adult

YELLOW-BILLED CUCKOO

Coccyzus americanus L 12" (31 cm)

FIELD MARKS

Gray-brown above, mostly white below; yellow orbital ring

Decurved bill with dark upper mandible and yellow lower

Undertail patterned in bold black and white

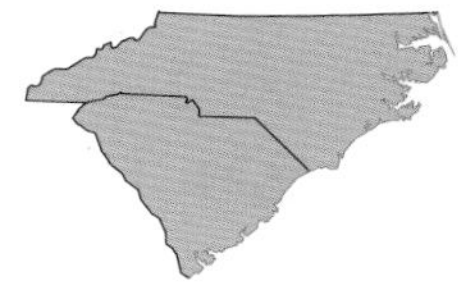

Behavior

This shy species slips quietly through woodlands, combing vegetation for caterpillars, frogs, lizards, and other insects. During courtship, male will climb on female's shoulders to feed her from above. Unique song sounds hollow and wooden, a rapid staccato *kuk-kuk-kuk*, usually descending to a *kakakowlp-kowlp* ending; it is often heard in the spring and summer.

Habitat

Common in dense canopies of woods, orchards, and streamside groves. Also inhabits tangles of swamp edges. Lines nest, located on horizontal tree limbs, with grasses and moss. Winters in South America.

Local Sites

This reclusive species visits dense woodlands throughout the Carolinas in summer. Look for it from Pisgah National Forest in the west to Croatan National Forest in the east and in wooded areas in between.

FIELD NOTES On Appalachian breeding grounds, the Black-billed Cuckoo, *Coccyzus erythropthalmus* (inset), is known to sometimes lay its eggs in the nests of Yellow-billeds. It is best distinguished by its dark bill and red eye ring.

Year-round | Adult

BARN OWL

Tyto alba L 16" (41 cm)

FIELD MARKS

White heart-shaped face

Dark eyes, pale bill

Rusty brown above, cinnamon-barred wings

White to pale cinnamon spotted underparts, darker on females

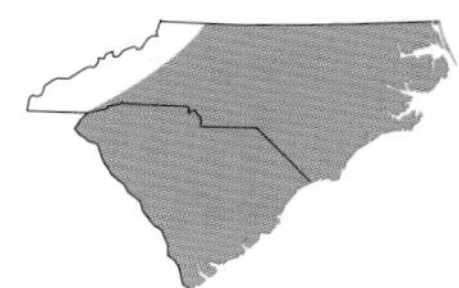

Behavior

A nocturnal forager of mice, small birds, bats, snakes, and insects. Hunts primarily by sound, often in pastures and marshes. Wing feathers with loosely knit edges and soft body plumage make its flight almost soundless, effective in surprising its prey. Roosts and nests in dark cavities in city and farm buildings, cliffs, and trees. Call is a harsh, raspy, hissing screech.

Habitat

Distributed throughout the world, this owl has adapted to the activities of man and is found in urban, suburban, rural, and forest regions throughout its range. Nests at all times of year in various sites, including tree hollows, barn rafters, burrows, or cliff holes.

Local Sites

Widespread throughout much of the Carolinas, the best spots to see Barn Owls are along the coast at sites such as Santee Coastal Reserve.

FIELD NOTES The Barn Owl is currently a declining species in the East, likely a victim of mechanized agriculture, which leaves little in the way of suitable hunting ground. Old barns being replaced by metal structures may also be a factor.

Year-round | Adult rufous morph

EASTERN SCREECH-OWL

Megascops asio L 8½" (22 cm)

FIELD MARKS

Small; with yellow eyes and pale tip on yellow-green bill

Underparts marked by vertical streaks crossed by dark bars

Ear tufts prominent if raised

Round, flattened facial disk

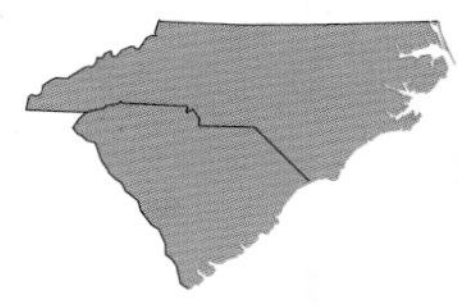

Behavior

Nocturnal; uses exceptional vision and hearing to hunt for mice, voles, shrews, and insects. If approached while roosting during the day, it will stretch its body, erect its ear tufts, and shut its eyes to blend into its background. Rufous, gray, and brown morphs exist, with the rufous and gray morphs seen with equal frequency in the Carolinas. Emits a series of quavering whistles, descending in pitch, or a long, one-pitch trill, most often heard in winter and spring.

Habitat

Common in a wide variety of habitats including woodlots, forests, swamps, orchards, parks, and suburban gardens. Nests in trees about 10 to 30 feet up.

Local Sites

Eastern Screech-Owls are year-round residents in the Carolinas at sites such as Francis Marion National Forest, Congaree National Park, and Weymouth Woods, as well as throughout the Appalachians.

FIELD NOTES Like most owls, the Eastern Screech-Owl seeks out the densest and thickest cover for its daytime roost. To find it, search the ground for regurgitated pellets of bone and fur, then look in the trees above. Also listen for small flocks of chickadees noisily mobbing a roosting owl. Small songbirds are often more likely to find an owl than you are.

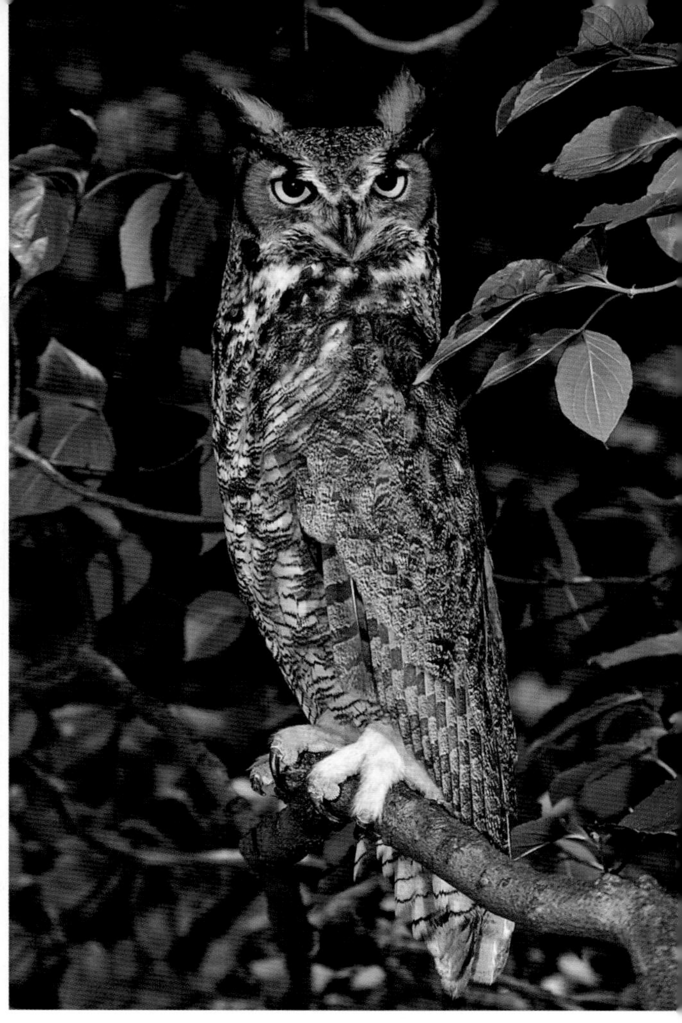

Year-round | Adult

GREAT HORNED OWL

Bubo virginianus L 22" (56 cm)

FIELD MARKS

Mottled brownish gray above, densely barred below

Long ear tufts (or "horns")

Rust-colored facial disks

Yellow eyes; white chin and throat; buff-colored underwings

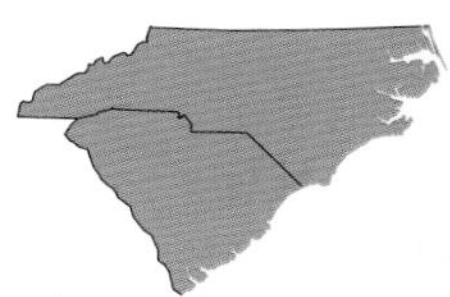

Behavior

Chiefly nocturnal. Feeds on a variety of animals including cats, skunks, porcupines, birds, snakes, and frogs; watches from high perch, then swoops down on prey. One of the earliest birds to nest, beginning in January or February, possibly to take advantage of winter-stressed prey. Call is a series of three to eight loud, deep hoots, the second and third often short and rapid.

Habitat

Found in a wide variety of habitats including forests, cities, and farmlands. Uses abandoned nests of other large birds, usually found in a tree.

Local Sites

Adaptable and widespread Great Horned Owls inhabit swamps of ACE Basin National Wildlife Refuge as well as peaks of Great Smoky Mountains National Park.

FIELD NOTES Only slightly smaller than the Great Horned, the Barred Owl, *Strix varia* (inset), also inhabits a variety of woodlands in the Carolinas. Its loud rhythmic call, *who-cooks-for-you, who-cooks-for-you-all*, is much more likely to be heard during the day than most owls' calls.

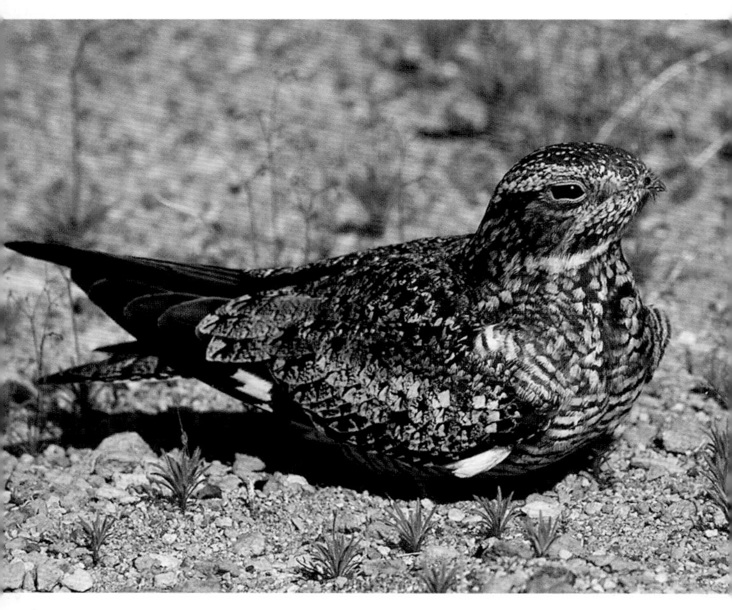

Year-round | Adult

COMMON NIGHTHAWK

Chordeiles minor L 9½" (24 cm)

FIELD MARKS

Dark gray-brown mottled back; bold white bar across primaries

Long, pointed wings with pale spotting; tail slightly forked

Underparts whitish with bold dusky bars; bar on tail in males

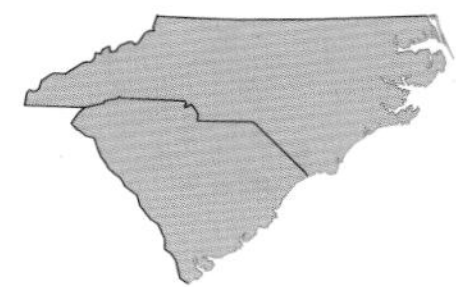

Behavior

The Common Nighthawk's streamlined body allows agile aerial displays when feeding at dusk. Hunts in flight, snaring insects. Drops lower jaw to create opening wide enough to scoop up large moths. Skims over surface of lakes to drink. Roosts on the ground, scraping a shallow depression, or on branches, posts, or roofs. Call is a nasal *peent.* Male's wings make hollow booming sound during diving courtship display.

Habitat

Frequents woodlands and shrubby areas; also seen in urban and suburban settings. Nests on the ground or on gravel rooftops.

Local Sites

Common Nighthawks are common, but declining, summer visitors to the Carolinas. Listen for their frog-like calls in wooded areas such as Carolina Sandhills National Wildlife Refuge and Croatan National Forest.

FIELD NOTES The Common Nighthawk only became common in towns and cities of North America in the mid-1800s with the development of flat, graveled roofs, which it could use to nest. Today it is seen regularly in summer swooping past street lights, snagging flying insects drawn to the outdoor luminescence.

Year-round | Adult

CHUCK-WILL'S-WIDOW

Caprimulgus carolinensis L 12" (31 cm)

FIELD MARKS

Buff-brown or grayish mottling overall; dark spotting on back

Long, rounded wings and tail

Whitish necklace; grayish eyebrow

In flight, male shows white on corners of tail feathers

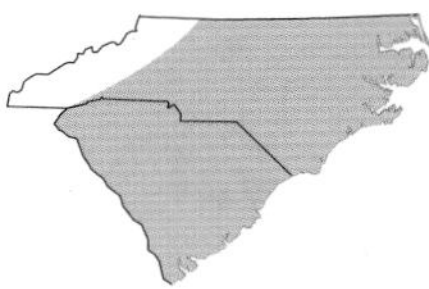

Behavior

Shy, the Chuck-will's-widow is not easily approached and will flush readily if disturbed, flitting away on silent wings. At night, flies low to the ground in search of insects. Roosts during the day perched on a limb or on the ground, where it is virtually impossible to see unless flushed. Often returns to the same perch every day. Song is unmistakable, an incessant, loud, whistled *chuck-will's-wid-ow*, with an emphasis on the third syllable. It can be heard throughout summer.

Habitat

Locally common in pine woodlands, live-oak groves, and other deciduous forests. Nests on the ground atop dry leaves with no nesting materials.

Local Sites

Wooded areas of the Carolinas, such as Francis Marion National Forest and Weymouth Woods, resound by night in summer with the Chuck-will's-widows' songs.

FIELD NOTES A nocturnal feeder, the Chuck-will's-widow can catch numerous insects on the same swoop in its two-inch wide mouth opening. Bristles in the corners of its mouth also aid in trapping prey. It is even known to sometimes take small birds, which it is able to swallow whole.

Year-round | Adult

CHIMNEY SWIFT

Chaetura pelagica L 5¼" (13 cm)

FIELD MARKS

Short, cigar-shaped body

Long, pointed, narrow wings

Dark plumage, sooty gray overall

Short, stubby tail

Blackish gray bill, legs, feet

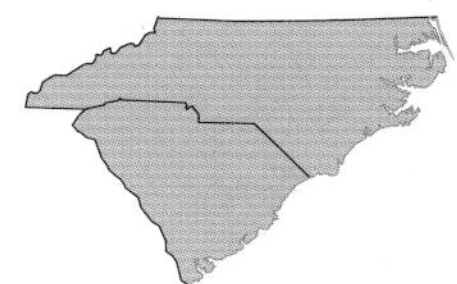

Behavior

Soars erratically on long wings at impressive speeds, snatching up ants, termites, and spiders while in flight. Look for large groups of Chimney Swifts circling above rooftops at dusk before dropping into chimneys to roost. During aerial courtship, the suitor raises its wings into a sharp V. Its call, given in flight, is a continual high-pitched chattering.

Habitat

Builds cup-shaped nests of small twigs glued together with dried saliva in chimneys, under eaves of abandoned barns, and in hollow trees. Roosts in chimneys and steeples. Otherwise seen soaring over forested, open, or urban sites. Winters as far south as Peru.

Local Sites

Chimney Swifts can be seen in summer circling in flocks at great speeds high over cities and towns throughout the Carolinas.

FIELD NOTES The Chimney Swift once confined its nests to tree hollows and other natural sites. Over the centuries, it has adapted so well to artificial nesting sites, such as chimneys, air shafts, vertical pipes, barns, and silos, that the species's numbers have increased dramatically. It is the only swift seen regularly in the eastern United States.

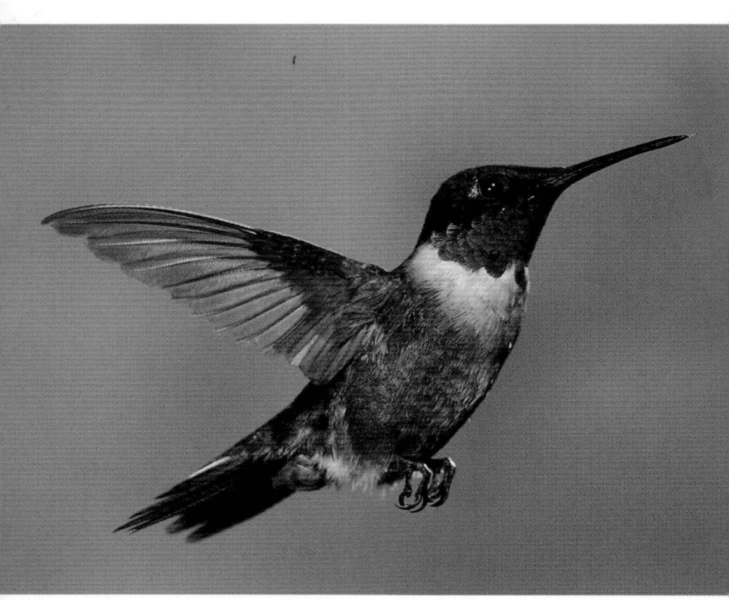

Year-round | Adult male

RUBY-THROATED HUMMINGBIRD

Archilochus colubris L 3¾" (10 cm)

FIELD MARKS

Metallic green above

Adult male has brilliant red gorget, black chin, whitish underparts, and dusky green sides

Female lacks gorget, has whitish throat and underparts, and a buffy wash on sides

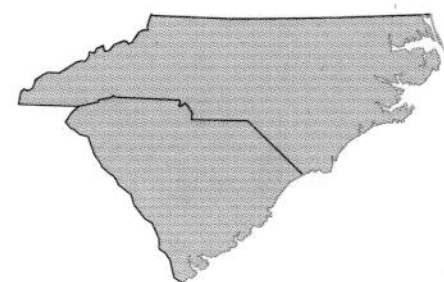

Behavior

Probes flowers and hummingbird feeders for nectar by hovering, virtually still, in midair. Also feeds on small spiders and insects. When nectar is scarce, known to drink sap from wells made in tree trunks by sapsuckers. In spring, male Ruby-throateds arrive in breeding territory before females and engage in jousts to claim prime territory. In addition to the hum generated by its rapidly beating wings, this bird emits soft *tchiv* notes.

Habitat

Found in gardens and woodland edges throughout most of the eastern United States. Female builds nest on small, downsloping tree limbs.

Local Sites

Find the Ruby-throated drinking from summer flowers or hummingbird feeders throughout the Carolinas.

FIELD NOTES The Rufous Hummingbird, *Selasphorus rufus* (inset: male), is a western species that is rare but regular in the Carolinas in late fall and winter. The proliferation of hummingbird feeders in backyard gardens may account for the recent increase in sightings.

Immature | Male

BELTED KINGFISHER

Ceryle alcyon L 13" (33 cm)

FIELD MARKS

Blue-gray head with large, shaggy crest

Blue-gray upperparts and breast band; white underparts and collar

Long, heavy, dark bill

Chestnut sides, belly band in female

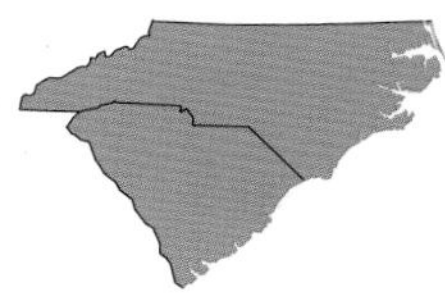

Behavior

Generally solitary and vocal, dives headfirst for fish from a waterside perch or after hovering above in order to line up on its target. Also feeds on insects, amphibians, and small reptiles. Both male and female carry out work in excavating nest tunnel, and share parenting duties. Mated pairs renew their relationship each breeding season with courtship rituals such as dramatic display flights, the male's feeding of the female, and vocalizations. Call is a loud, dry rattle; given when alarmed, to announce territory, or while in flight.

Habitat

Conspicuous along rivers, ponds, lakes, and coastal estuaries. Prefers partially wooded areas. Monogamous pairs nest in burrows they dig three or more feet into vertical earthen banks near watery habitats.

Local Sites

Belted Kingfishers can be found year-round diving for fish in the rivers and ponds of wetland sites such as ACE Basin, Santee, Mattamuskeet, and Alligator River National Wildlife Refuges.

FIELD NOTES The Belted Kingfisher female is one of the few in North America that is more colorful than her male counterpart, which lacks the female's chestnut band across the belly and chestnut sides and flanks.

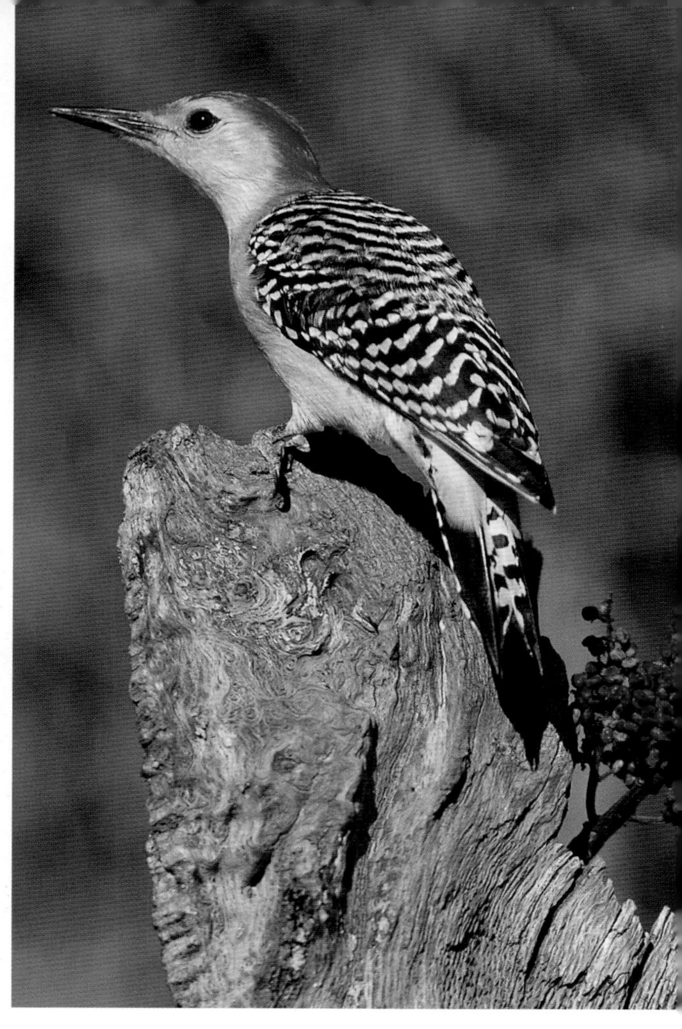

Year-round | Adult male

RED-BELLIED WOODPECKER

Melanerpes carolinus L 9¼" (24 cm)

FIELD MARKS

Black-and-white barred back

Red nape, extending onto crown only on males

Mostly grayish underparts; small reddish tinge on belly

Central tail feathers barred

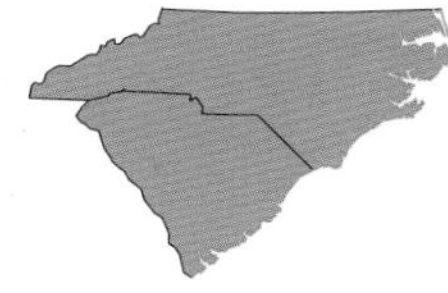

Behavior

Climbs tree trunks by bracing itself with stiff tail, taking strain off short legs. Uses chisel-shaped bill to drill cavities in tree bark for nest holes or to extract grubs and insects. Also feeds on worms, fruits, seeds, sap from wells made by sapsuckers, and on sunflower seeds and peanut butter at feeders. Call is a whirring *churr* or *chiv-chiv* that rises and falls, reminiscent of the whirring of wings.

Habitat

Common in open woodlands, forest edges, suburbs, and parks. Nests and roosts at night in tree cavities.

Local Sites

Widespread and common in the Carolinas, look for Red-bellieds from the forests of the Appalachians to woodlands lining the coast.

FIELD NOTES The Yellow-bellied Sapsucker, *Sphyrapicus varius* (inset), is a winter visitor to woodlands throughout most of the Carolinas. It drills rows of small holes in tree trunks to feed off the sap produced and the insects attracted. Species such as the Red-bellied Woodpecker, the Ruby-throated Hummingbird, kinglets, and others also visit these wells for an easy snack.

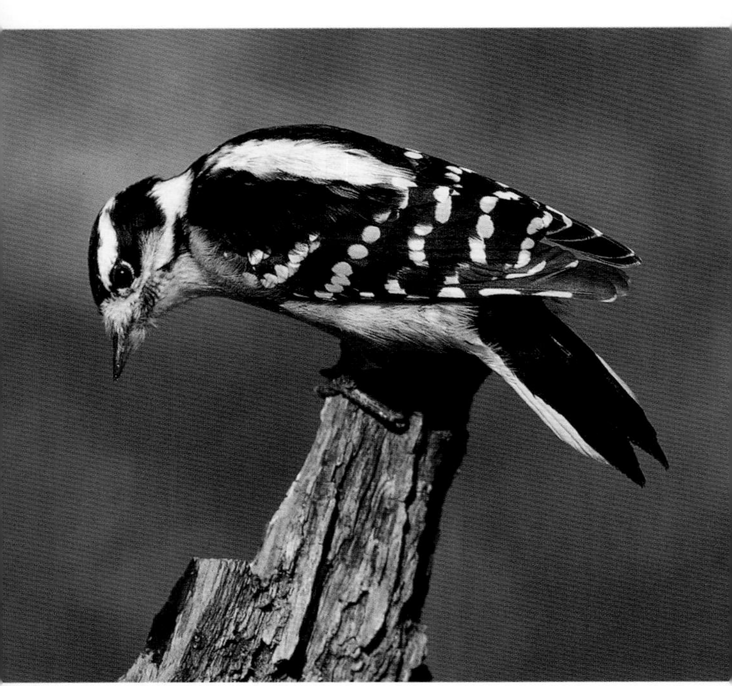

Year-round | Adult female

DOWNY WOODPECKER

Picoides pubescens L 6¾" (17 cm)

FIELD MARKS

Black cap, ear patch, moustachial stripe; black wings spotted white

Block of white on back

White tuft in front of eyes; white underparts

Red occipital patch on male only

Behavior

The smallest woodpecker in North America, it forages mainly on insects, larvae, and eggs. Readily visits backyard feeders for sunflower seeds and suet. Will also consume poison ivy berries. Small size enables Downy to forage on smaller, thinner limbs. Both male and female stake territorial claims with their drumming. Call is a high-pitched but soft *pik.*

Habitat

Common in suburbs, parks, and orchards, as well as forests and woodlands. Nests in cavities of dead trees.

Local Sites

Widespread throughout the Carolinas, but can be difficult to locate in dense woods, Downy Woodpeckers are known to frequent backyard feeding stations.

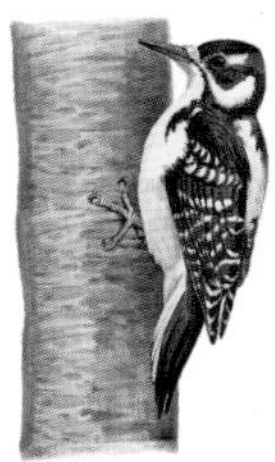

FIELD NOTES The larger and less common Hairy Woodpecker, *Picoides villosus* (inset), is similarly marked but has a bill as long as its head and a sharper, louder, lower-pitched call. It also tends to stay on tree trunks or larger limbs than the Downy. Note the all-white outer tail feathers of the Hairy Woodpecker; the Downy's outer tail feathers are often barred or spotted black.

Year-round | Adult

RED-COCKADED WOODPECKER

Picoides borealis L 8½" (22 cm)

FIELD MARKS

Black-and-white barred back; Black forehead, cap, and nape

Large white cheek patches; whitish underparts with barred and spotted flanks

Red tufts, often concealed, on male's head behind eyes

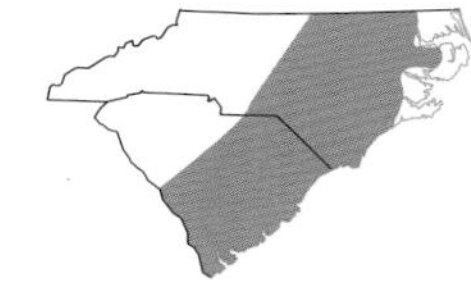

Behavior

This endangered species forages for insects by drilling into pine trunks, sometimes moving up trunk in spiral fashion. Also feeds on berries and nuts. A cooperative breeder, the Red-cockaded is often seen in a cluster of three to seven, consisting of a mated pair, nestlings, and unmated helper adults. Calls include a buzzy, raspy *sripp* and a high-pitched *tsick*.

Habitat

Inhabits open, mature pine or pine-oak woodlands where unlogged stands of 80- to 90-year-old trees still remain. Requires a living pine afflicted with heartwood disease for nesting, as pine pitch produced by drill holes presumably repels predators such as snakes.

Local Sites

Carolina Sandhills National Wildlife Refuge was established to protect the Red-cockaded population there.

FIELD NOTES The male Red-cockaded bores his nest hole into a living pine. He then drills small holes around the nest opening to gain a good flow of sap. In all, it takes him more than a year to complete, but the hole can be used for another 50 years by a variety of other animals including birds, squirrels, mice, and insects. These cavities also serve as distinctive signposts for humans in search of this elusive species.

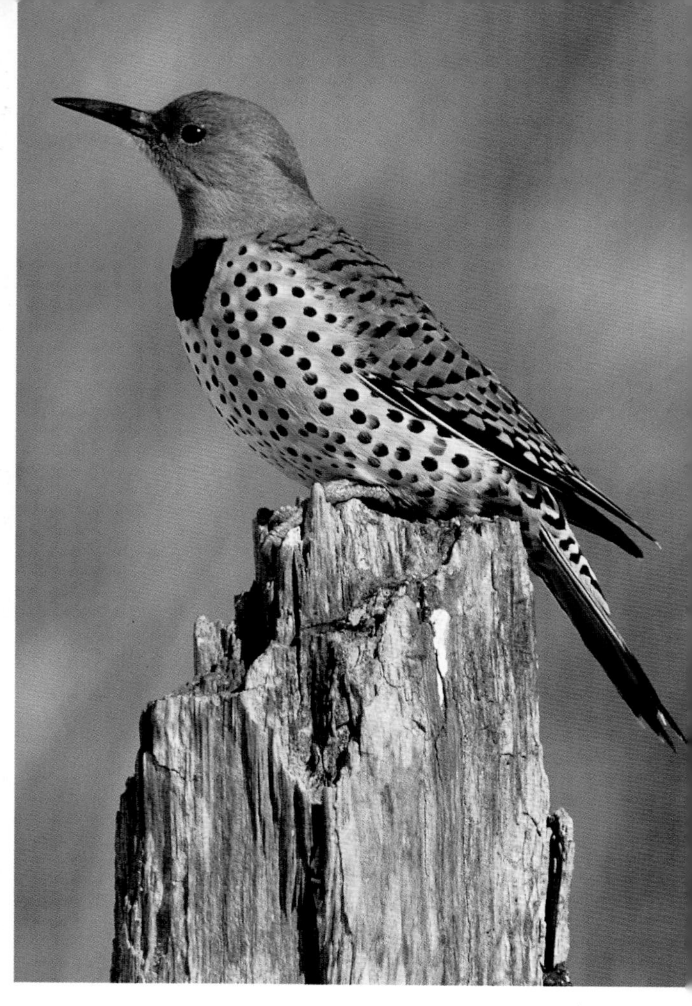

Year-round | Adult female "Yellow-shafted"

NORTHERN FLICKER

Colaptes auratus L 12½" (32 cm)

FIELD MARKS

White rump, yellowish underwing

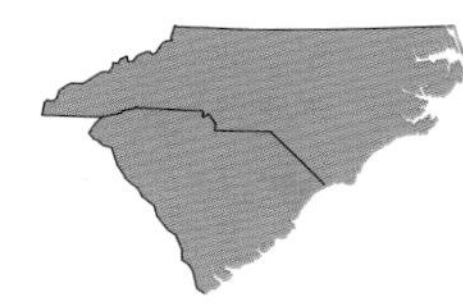

Brown, barred back, cream underparts with black spotting, and black crescent bib

Gray crown, tan face, red crescent on nape, and, on male, black moustachial stripe

Behavior

Feeds mostly on the ground, foraging primarily for ants. A cavity-nesting bird, the flicker will drill into wooden surfaces, including utility poles and houses. Bows to its partner before engaging in a courtship dance of exaggerated wing and tail movements. Call is a long, loud series of *wick-er, wick-er* during breeding season, or a single, loud *klee-yer* heard year-round.

Habitat

Prefers open woodlands and suburban areas with sizeable living and dead trees. An insectivore, the Northern Flicker is at least partially migratory, traveling in the winter in pursuit of food.

Local Sites

Widespread and common, flickers can be found wherever there are ants, mostly in wooded areas, but also in towns and cities.

FIELD NOTES The larger, darker, and less common Pileated Woodpecker, *Dryocopus pileatus* (inset), also has quite a penchant for ants. It forages low on trees or on fallen logs, leaving behind a distinctive rectangular hole. It is distributed in hardwood forests throughout the Carolinas.

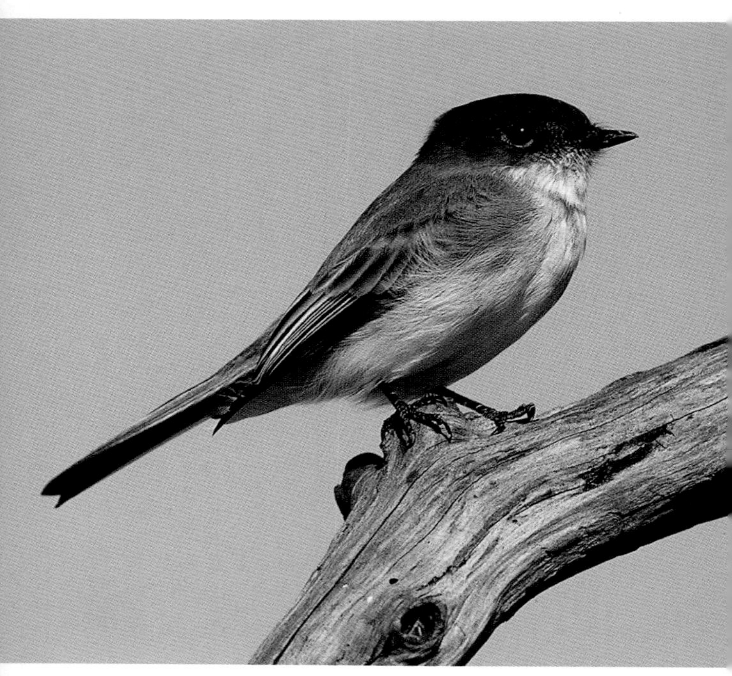

Year-round | Adult

EASTERN PHOEBE

Sayornis phoebe L 7" (18 cm)

FIELD MARKS

Brownish gray above, darkest on head, wings, and tail; dark bill; lacks wing bars

Underparts mostly white with pale olive wash on sides and breast

Fresh fall birds washed with yellow on belly

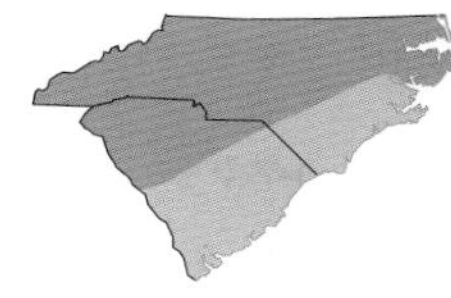

Behavior

The Eastern Phoebe flicks its tail constantly when perched, looking for flying insects to chase and snare in midair. Also easts small fish, berries, and fruit. It is among the first birds to migrate each spring. Its distinctive eponymous song is a harsh, emphatic *fee-be,* accented on the first syllable; often repeated when male is attempting to lure a mate. Call is a sharp *chip.*

Habitat

Common in woodlands, farmlands, and suburbs. Often builds delicate cup-like nest under bridges, in eaves, and in rafters, often near running water.

Local Sites

Eastern Phoebes can be found year-round giving chase to insects flying over the streams of Walhalla State Fish Hatchery in Sumter National Forest.

FIELD NOTES Though very similarly plumaged, the Eastern Phoebe is distinguished from the Eastern Wood-Pewee, *Contopus virens* (inset), by its habit of constantly pumping its tail when perched. The Wood-Pewee tends to perch motionless for quite a long time. Moreover the Wood-Pewee's lower mandible is a dull orange and it has two thin whitish wing bars.

Year-round | Adult

EASTERN KINGBIRD

Tyrannus tyrannus L 8½" (22 cm)

FIELD MARKS

Black head, slate gray back

White terminal band on black tail

Underparts white, pale gray wash across breast

Orange-red crown patch visible only when displaying

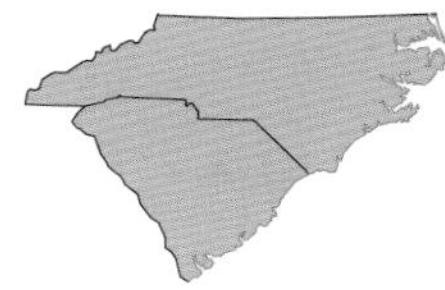

Behavior

Waits on perch until it spots prey, then darts to snare it in midair. Feeds during summer primarily on flying insects. May also hover to pick food off ground. Males court with erratic hovering, swooping, and circling, revealing otherwise hidden crown patch. Aggressively defends its nest against considerably larger birds. Raspy call when feeding or defending sounds like *zeer;* also uses a harsh *dzeet* note alone or in a series.

Habitat

Common and conspicuous in woodland clearings, farms, orchards, and field edges. Builds cup-shaped nest near the end of a horizontal tree branch, sometimes on a post or stump. Winters in South America.

Local Sites

Look throughout the Carolinas in summer for the Kingbird's precise aerial manuevers; Croatan National Forest is one good spot.

FIELD NOTES Another summer migrant to woodlands of the Carolinas from the *Tyrannidae* family is the Great Crested Flycatcher, *Myiarchus crinitus* (inset). It tends to more densely wooded areas than the kingbird and often remains hidden toward the tops of tall trees. Listen in summer for its distinctive call, a loud, whistled *wheep*.

Year-round | Adult

WHITE-EYED VIREO

Vireo griseus L 5" (13 cm)

FIELD MARKS

Grayish olive above

White neck and belly; pale yellow sides and flanks

Yellow spectacles; distinctive white iris visible at close range

Two whitish wing bars

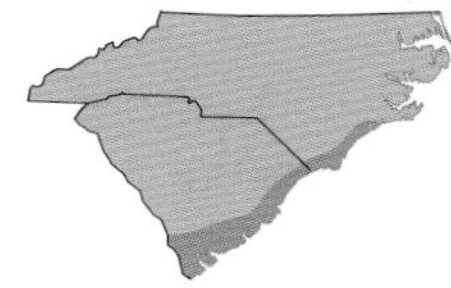

Behavior

Usually seen by itself, its thick, blunt, slightly hooked bill is used for catching flies and picking fruits and berries. Known to sing into the heat of summer, the White-eyed Vireo is characterized by a loud, grating, jumbled, five- to seven-note call, usually beginning and ending with a sharp *chick*. The notes run together, the middle portion seeming to mimic other birds' songs. Regional and individual variations abound, but the standard, generic sequence is *quick-with-the-beer-check!*

Habitat

Prefers to conceal itself close to the ground in dense thickets, brushy tangles, and forest undergrowth. Nest located close to the ground in shrub or small tree.

Local Sites

Found year-round on the coast north to Onslow Bay, White-eyed Vireos are summer residents of the rest of the Carolinas.

FIELD NOTES With an olive back, a white belly, and yellow spectacles, the Yellow-throated Vireo, *Vireo flavifrons* (inset), can be distinguished by its bright yellow throat and chin, and at close range, by its dark irises. It also tends to forage much higher up in trees than the White-eyed.

Year-round | Adult

BLUE-HEADED VIREO

Vireo solitarius L 5" (13 cm)

FIELD MARKS

Solid blue-gray hood contrasts with white spectacles and throat

Olive or bluish back; yellow sides and flanks sometimes greenish

Prominent wing bars and tertial edges; white on outer tail feathers

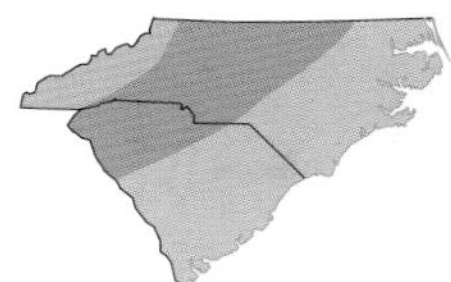

Behavior

Most often by itself or in a pair, the Blue-headed is the first vireo to return to its Appalachian breeding grounds in spring. Forages on branches and treetops for insects and sometimes fruit. May also give chase to a flying insect or hover to pick one off foliage. Courtship display involves much singing, bobbing, and showcasing of yellow flank feathers by the male. Song is a slow, drawn-out, sometimes slurred *cheerio-cheree-sissy-a-wit*, heard frequently throughout the day.

Habitat

Common in mixed woodlands, where it stays primarily in higher branches. Nests in forks of trees or bushes.

Local Sites

The Carolinas hosts two subspecies of Blue-headed Vireo. One breeds in the Appalachians and has a bluish back and a thick bill. The other winters on the coastal plain and has an olive back and a thinner bill.

FIELD NOTES The song of the Red-eyed Vireo, *Vireo olivaceus* (inset: adult, left; immature, right), is similar to the Blue-headed's, but quicker and more repetitive. By sight, the Red-eyed is clearly set apart by its distinct white eyebrow, bordered in black, and by its lack of wing bars.

Year-round | Adult

BLUE JAY

Cyanocitta cristata L 11" (28 cm)

FIELD MARKS

Blue crest and back

Black barring and white patches on blue wings and tail

Black collar line on grayish underparts extends onto nape

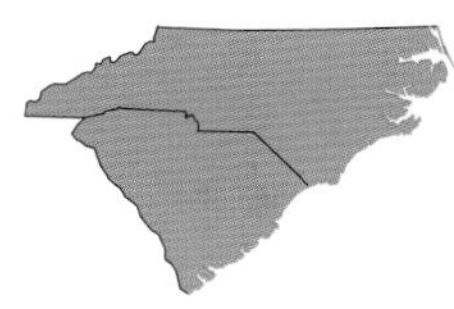

Behavior

Often seen in small family groups, foraging for insects, acorns, nuts, berries, and seeds. Blue Jays are also known to raid nests for eggs and nestlings of other species. A two-note vocalization and a bobbing display may be observed during courtship. Noisy, bold Blue Jays are noted for their loud, piercing alarm call of *jay-jay-jay,* their musical *weedle-eedle,* and their imitations of several hawk species.

Habitat

The Blue Jay has adapted to fragmented woodlands, parks, and suburban backyards. Builds nest in oak and beech trees 5 to 20 feet up. Some birds are migratory, while others are year-round residents.

Local Sites

Common year-round across the Carolinas, Blue Jays often favor areas with an abundance of acorns.

FIELD NOTES A resourceful feeder, the Blue Jay will store acorns in the ground for winter months when food is scarce. As many of these acorns are never recovered, this practice is a major factor in the establishment and distribution of oak forests throughout the jay's range.

Year-round | Adult

AMERICAN CROW

Corvus brachyrhynchos L 17½" (45 cm)

FIELD MARKS

Black, iridescent plumage overall

Broad wings and fan-shaped tail

Long, heavy, black bill

Brown eyes

Black legs and feet

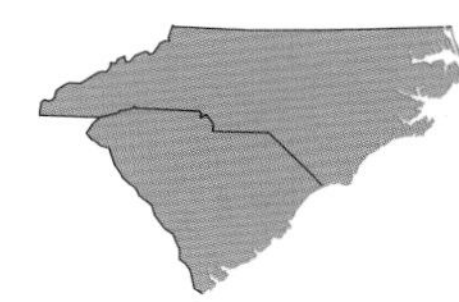

Behavior

Omnivorous, this crow often forages, roosts, and travels in flocks. Individuals take turns at sentry duty while others feed on insects, garbage, grain, mice, eggs, and baby birds. Regularly seen noisily mobbing large raptors such as eagles, hawks, and Great Horned Owls. Because its bill is ineffective on tough hides, crows wait for another predator—or an automobile—to open a carcass before dining. Studies have shown the crow's ability to count, solve puzzles, and retain information. Readily identified by its familiar call, *caw-caw.*

Habitat

Among the most widely distributed and familiar birds in North America. Lives in a variety of habitats.

Local Sites

Widespread throughout the Carolinas, crows can be seen almost everywhere, from farm fields to cities.

FIELD NOTES The very similar Fish Crow, *Corvus ossifragus* (inset), is smaller than the American Crow, but is best told apart by its high, nasal, two-syllable *ca-hah* call. It is found on the coastal plain of the Carolinas.

Year-round | Adult male

PURPLE MARTIN

Progne subis L 8" (20 cm)

FIELD MARKS

Male is dark, glossy purplish blue

Female has bluish gray upperparts; grayish breast and belly

Long, pointed wings; forked tail

Dark eyes, bill, legs, and feet

Juvenile brown above, gray below

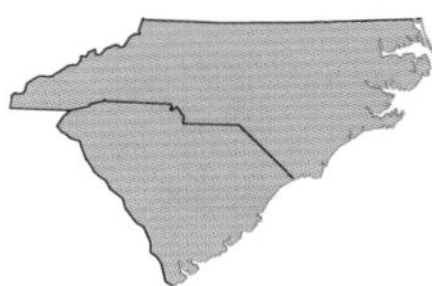

Behavior

Forages almost exclusively in flight, darting for wasps, bees, dragonflies, winged ants, and other large insects. Long, sharply pointed wings and substantial tail allow it graceful maneuverability in the air. Capable of drinking, even bathing, in flight by skimming just over water's surface and dipping bill, or breast, into water. Song is a series of liquid, gurgling notes.

Habitat

Common in summer in open habitat near water where it nests almost exclusively in man-made multi-dwelling martin houses. Winters in South America.

Local Sites

One of the largest roost sites of martins in the East is on Lunch Island in Lake Murray, South Carolina, following breeding but before migration, when hundreds of thousands of birds darken the sky there.

FIELD NOTES Purple Martins in the eastern half of their range are highly dependent on man-made nesting houses, which can hold many pairs of breeding adults. The tradition of making martin houses from hollowed gourds originated with Native Americans, who found that this sociable bird helped reduce insects around villages and crops. The practice was adopted by colonists, and martins have accordingly prospered for many generations.

Year-round | Adult

TREE SWALLOW

Tachycineta bicolor L 5¾" (15 cm)

FIELD MARKS

Dark, glossy, greenish blue above; white below

Slightly notched tail

Long, pointed, blackish wings

Juvenile gray-brown above

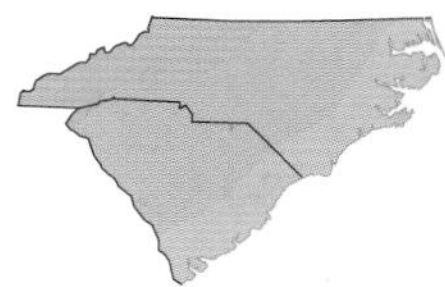

Behavior

Abundant and widespread, with uncanny ability to adapt to divergent environments. Often seen in huge flocks, especially during fall migration, or perched in long rows on branches and wires. Darts over fields or water to catch insects in flight, but changes to a diet of berries or plant buds during colder months, when insects are less abundant. The Tree Swallow even preens itself in flight. Song is a rapid, repeated *chi-veet.*

Habitat

Common to wooded habitats near water, or where dead trees provide nest holes in fields, marshes, or towns. Also nests in fence posts, barn eaves, and man-made birdhouses.

Local Sites

Savannah National Wildlife Refuge is a beautiful area in which to find Tree Swallows in winter.

FIELD NOTES Once Tree Swallows leave most of the Carolinas' coastal plain in spring, look for Northern Rough-winged Swallows, *Stelgidopteryx serripennis* (inset), to take their place. They have a similar size and body type, but are duskier brown above and do not show as much contrast between dark head and paler neck and breast.

Year-round | Adult

BARN SWALLOW

Hirundo rustica L 6¾" (17 cm)

FIELD MARKS

Long, deeply forked, dark tail with white spotting

Iridescent blue upperparts

Cinnamon to buff underparts

Rusty brown forehead and throat; dark blue-black breast band

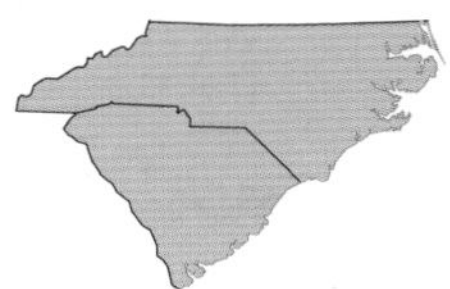

Behavior

An exuberant flyer, the Barn Swallow is often seen in small flocks skimming low over the surface of a field or pond, taking insects in midair. Will follow tractors and lawn mowers to feed on flushed insects, many of which are harmful to crops. An indicator of coming storms, as barometric pressure changes cause the bird to fly lower to the ground. Call is a short, repeated *wit-wit.*

Habitat

Frequents open farms and fields, especially near water. Has adapted to humans to the extent that it now nests almost exclusively in structures such as barns, bridges, culverts, and garages. Winters in South America.

Local Sites

Barn Swallows can be found along streams throughout the Carolinas as early as April. Jordan and Falls Lakes are both fairly reliable spots in summer.

FIELD NOTES The Cliff Swallow, *Petrochelidon pyrrhonota* (inset), can also be found in summer nesting under bridges and eaves or foraging over fields and ponds. In flight, it is best distinguished from the Barn Swallow by its squarish tail and buffy rump. Its whitish forehead is a distinctive field mark as well.

Breeding | Adult

CAROLINA CHICKADEE

Poecile carolinensis L 4¾" (12 cm)

FIELD MARKS

Black cap and bib

White cheeks, gray upperparts

Whitish underparts,with buff-gray wash on flanks and lower belly, most evident in fall

Short black bill, short notched tail

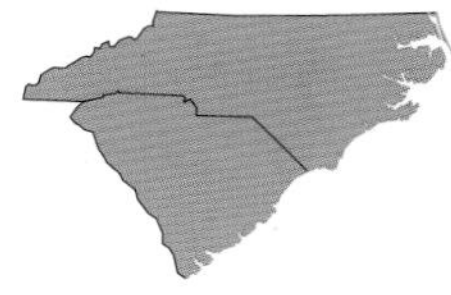

Behavior

Seldom descends to ground, energetically foraging among leaves and twigs for moths, caterpillars, and insects. May hang upside down to glean underside of foliage. Visits backyard feeders for seeds and suet. If disturbed at the nest, will strike or hiss at intruder in a snake-like fashion. Call is a high-pitched, rapid *chick-a-dee-dee-dee.* Song is a four-note whistle, *fee-bee fee-bay.*

Habitat

Woodland edges and clearings, oak forests, wooded city parks, and suburban yards. Nests in old woodpecker holes, man-made nesting boxes, and natural crevices.

Local Sites

Carolina Chickadees are common year-round residents throughout the whole of the Carolinas. Look for them flitting about mid-level branches in woodlands of the Appalachians, the piedmont, and the coastal plain.

FIELD NOTES After breeding season, the Carolina Chickadee will often join in mixed foraging flocks with nuthatches, titmice, Downy Woodpeckers, kinglets, and other small birds. Look for these species in a loose group flitting from tree to tree as they comb through the trunks and vegetation of a patch of woods.

Year-round | Adult

TUFTED TITMOUSE

Baeolophus bicolor L 6¼" (16 cm)

FIELD MARKS

Gray crest; blackish forehead

Gray above, whitish below

Russet wash on sides

Pale spot around eyes

Juvenile has brownish forehead and pale crest

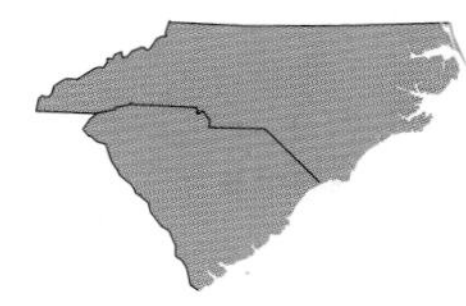

Behavior

Very active forager in trees, seeking insects, spiders, snails, berries, or seeds, sometimes hanging upside down to feed. May also be seen holding a nut with its feet and pounding it with its bill. A common visitor to backyard feeders, especially fond of sunflower seeds and suet. Stores surplus food underground. Male feeds female in courtship. Primary song is a loud, whistled *peter-peter-peter*, but it also employs up to ten other calls, which it uses to keep foraging groups together.

Habitat

Open forests, woodlands, groves, and orchards, as well as urban and suburban parks with large trees and shrubs. Nests in natural cavities, woodpecker holes, man-made boxes, and sometimes in fence posts.

Local Sites

Listen for the noisy calls of Tufted Titmice in wooded areas throughout the Carolinas, especially in Francis Marion and Croatan National Forests.

FIELD NOTES Unintimidated by proximity to humans, the Tufted Titmouse will approach people who make a squeaking sound or *pish*, a useful tool for a birder. It is even known to swoop down and pluck hair directly from a human's scalp for use in its nest.

Year-round | Adult

WHITE-BREASTED NUTHATCH

Sitta carolinensis L 5¾" (15 cm)

FIELD MARKS

White face and breast; black cap

Blue-gray upperparts; wing and tail feathers tipped in white

Rust or brown colored underparts near legs

White pattern on blue-black tail

Behavior

Creeps down tree trunks or large branches in search of insects or spiders. Will also gather nuts and seeds, jam them into bark, and hammer or "hatch" the food open with bill. Roosts in tree cavities, and sometimes even in crevices of bark in summer. Song of the White-breasted is typically a rapid series of nasal whistles on one pitch; call is usually a low-pitched, repeated, nasal *yank*.

Habitat

Prefers leafy trees in deciduous or mixed woods for foraging and nesting; builds nest in abandoned woodpecker holes or in natural cavities inside decaying trees.

Local Sites

Widespread year-round residents across the Carolinas, White-breasteds are found in wooded areas including Congaree and Great Smoky Mountains National Parks.

FIELD NOTES In winter, the White-breasted often joins mixed-species foraging groups with the Red-breasted Nuthatch, *Sitta canadensis* (inset: female, top; male, bottom). Though similar in behavior, the less common Red-breasted is noticeably smaller and has rust-colored underparts, darker on the males. The Red-breasted forages on small branches and outer twigs.

Year-round | Adult

BROWN-HEADED NUTHATCH

Sitta pusilla L 4½" (11 cm)

FIELD MARKS

Brown cap; pale nape spot

Blue-gray above, dull buff below

White cheeks, chin, and throat

Dark, narrow eyeline borders cap

Straight black bill

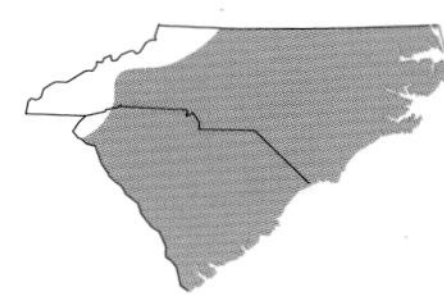

Behavior

A small and usually noisy nuthatch that feeds in pairs or small flocks. One of the few bird species known to use tools, forages in pine tree bark for insects, using one piece of bark to dislodge another. Also consumes large numbers of seeds from pinecones when insects are scarce. Forms flocks with chickadees, warblers, and other small landbirds. Call is a repeated double note like the squeak of a rubber duck. Feeding flocks also give twittering, chirping *bit bit bit* calls.

Habitat

Fairly widespread and locally common in pine woodlands and pine plantations. Nests in hollow trees, stumps, or man-made bird boxes.

Local Sites

This southeastern specialty can be found in pine woods throughout the Carolinas except on the highest of the Appalachian ridges. Look for it in Francis Marion or Croatan National Forests.

FIELD NOTES Though it scours tree trunks for insects in a very nuthatch-like fashion, the Brown Creeper, *Certhia americana* (inset), is actually in a family of its own. Camouflaged by streaked brown plumage, it quickly spirals up one tree trunk, then flies down to the bottom of another and spirals up again.

Year-round | Adult

CAROLINA WREN

Thryothorus ludovicianus L 5½" (14 cm)

FIELD MARKS

Deep rusty brown above with dark brown bars

Prominent white eye stripe

Warm buff below

White chin and throat

Long, slightly decurved bill

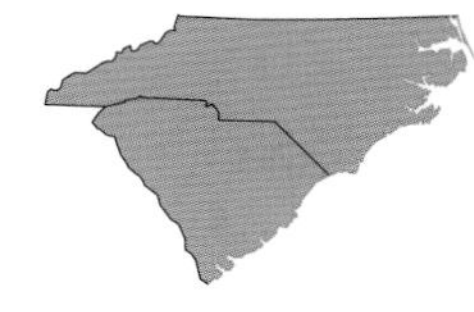

Behavior

South Carolina's state bird, it pokes around on the ground with its decurved bill, looking for insects, spiders, snails, fruits, berries, and seeds. May also eat small lizards and tree frogs. A pair stays together in its territory throughout the year. From its perch at any time of day or season, male sings melodious *tea-kettle tea-kettle tea-kettle* or *cheery-cheery-cheery,* to which female may respond with a growl of *t-shihrrr.*

Habitat

Generally remains concealed in underbrush of moist woodlands and swamps, and around human habitation on farms and in wooded suburbs. Nests in open cavities of suitable size, including woodpecker holes, barn rafters, mailboxes, flowerpots, even boots left outside.

Local Sites

The Carolina Wren's vivacious, liquid song can be heard year-round in any region of the Carolinas.

FIELD NOTES The northern limit of the Carolina Wren's range will expand and contract in response to the severity of winter weather. In mild years, it sometimes extends its range into Canada, but is pushed back by the next harsh winter.

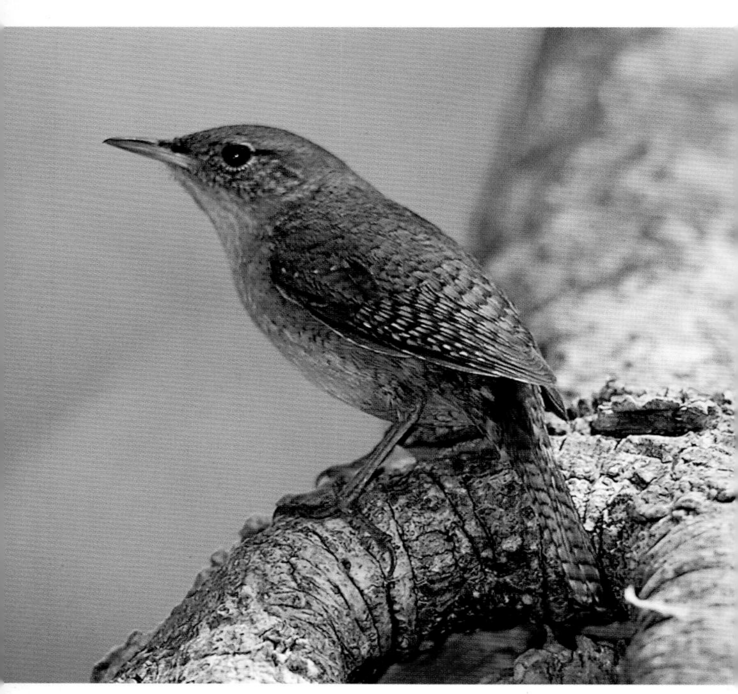

Year-round | Adult

HOUSE WREN

Troglodytes aedon L 4¾" (12 cm)

FIELD MARKS

Grayish or brown upperparts

Fine black barring on wings and tail

Pale gray underparts

Pale faint orbital ring, eyebrow

Thin, slightly decurved bill

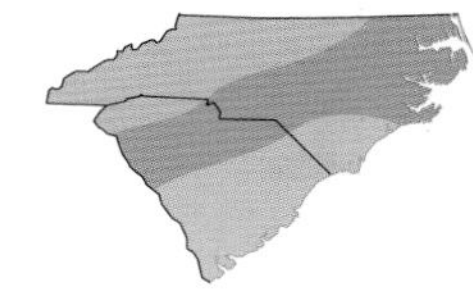

Behavior

Noisy, conspicuous, and relatively tame, with a tail often cocked upward. Gleans insects and spiders from vegetation. While most species of wren forage low to the ground, the House Wren will seek food at a variety of levels, including high in the trees. Sings exuberantly in a cascade of bubbling, whistled notes. Call is a rough *chek-chek,* often running into a chatter.

Habitat

Highly tolerant of human presence, hence common in shrubbery around farms, parks, and urban gardens. Nests in any cavity of suitable size.

Local Sites

This common visitor to backyard birdhouses is fairly easy to spot or hear in most suburban areas. Look for it as well in more heavily wooded regions from the coast to the mountains of the Carolinas.

FIELD NOTES Having pushed its breeding range south through most of the 1900s, the House Wren can now be found nesting throughout much of the Carolinas. The male begins construction on a number of possible nests, in crevices ranging from tree cavities to nesting boxes to mailboxes, even empty cans. A female joins him, inspects the nests, and chooses one to complete.

Year-round | Adult male

RUBY-CROWNED KINGLET

Regulus calendula L 4¼" (11 cm)

FIELD MARKS

Olive green above; dusky below

Yellow-edged plumage on wings

Two white wing bars

Short black bill; white eye ring

Male's red crown patch seldom visible except when agitated

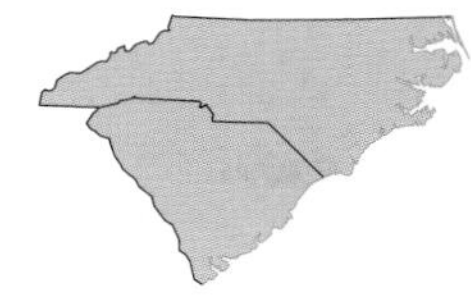

Behavior

A winter visitor, often forages in mixed-species flocks. Flicks its wings frequently as it searches for insects and their eggs or larvae on tree trunks, branches, and foliage. May also give chase to flying insects or glean those attracted to sap from tree wells drilled by sapsuckers. Calls include a scolding *ji-dit;* song consists of several high, thin *tsee* notes, followed by descending *tew* notes, ending with a trilled three-note phrase.

Habitat

Common in coniferous and mixed woodlands and in brushy thickets. Highly migratory.

Local Sites

In winter, look high in the trees of woodlands throughout the Carolinas for these energetic little songbirds.

FIELD NOTES A close relative of the Ruby-crowned, the Golden-crowned Kinglet, *Regulus satrapa* (inset), can be found in winter as it forages high up in trees. The Golden-crowned is set apart by its yellow crown patch and its white eyebrow stripe. The male (inset, bottom) has a brilliant orange tuft within his yellow crown patch.

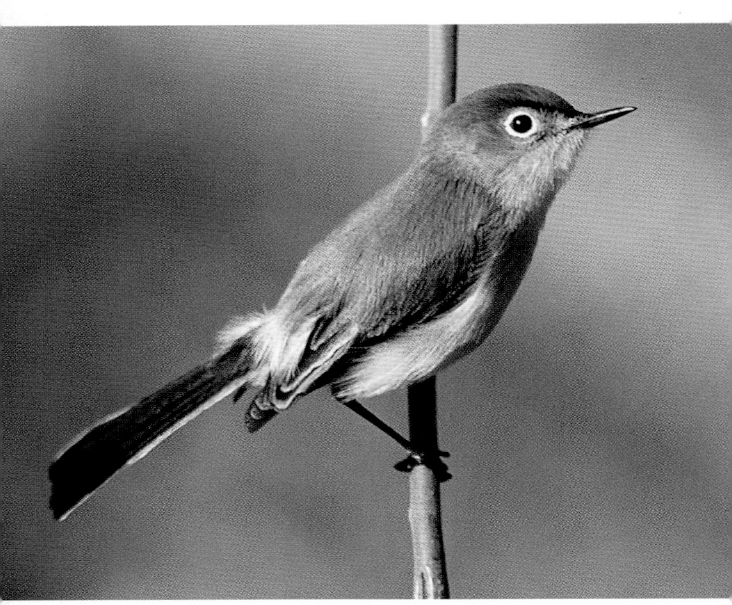

Breeding | Adult male

BLUE-GRAY GNATCATCHER

Polioptila caerulea L 4¼" (11 cm)

FIELD MARKS

Male is blue-gray above, female grayer; both are white below

Long, black tail with white outer feathers

Black forehead and eyebrow on male in breeding plumage

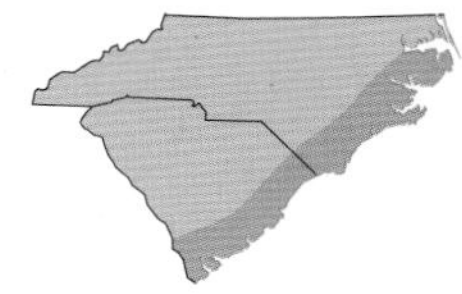

Behavior

Often seen near branch tips, the Blue-gray Gnatcatcher scours deciduous tree limbs and leaves for small insects, spiders, eggs, and larvae. Sometimes captures prey in flight and may hover briefly. Emits a querulous *pwee,* intoned like a question, as well as a high-pitched buzz. Known to imitate other birds' songs as well, a surprise to birders expecting this only from mocking-birds and thrashers.

Habitat

Favors moist woodlands and thickets. Male and female together make cup-like nest of plant fibers, spider webs, moss, and lichens on a branch or fork of a tree.

Local Sites

Blue-gray Gnatcatchers often nest near lakes and streams throughout the Carolinas. Listen for their high-pitched buzzing year-round at coastal sites like Francis Marion and Croatan National Forests.

FIELD NOTES Like many of the smaller songbird species, gnat-catchers hatch altricial—naked and unable to see, requiring complete parental care. Young are fed in the nest for about two weeks, then outside for an additional period of time. Avoid disturbing a nest site, as it may sometimes cause the couple to abandon it and rebuild elsewhere.

Year-round | Adult male

EASTERN BLUEBIRD

Sialia sialis L 7" (18 cm)

FIELD MARKS

Male is bright blue above

Chestnut throat, breast, flanks, and sides of neck

Female is a grayer blue above, duller below

White belly and undertail coverts

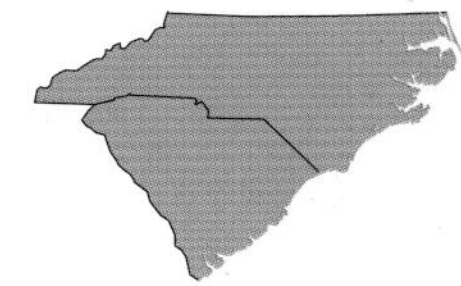

Behavior

Hunts from an elevated perch in the open, dropping to the ground to seize crickets, grasshoppers, and spiders. Has been observed pouncing on prey it has spotted from as much as 130 feet away. In winter, forms small flocks and roosts communally at night in tree cavities or nest boxes. During courtship, male shows vivid coloring on his side during wing-waving displays beside a chosen nesting site. Call is a musical, rising *chur-lee*, extended in song to *chur chur-lee chur-lee.*

Habitat

Found in open woodlands, meadows, farmlands, and orchards. Nests in woodpecker holes, hollow trees or stumps, and in nest boxes.

Local Sites

Eastern Bluebirds can be found year-round throughout the Carolinas. In winter, look for small flocks among scattered suburban woodlands or larger forests.

FIELD NOTES The Eastern Bluebird's serious decline in recent decades is due largely to competition for nesting sites with two introduced species, the European Starling and the House Sparrow. Specially designed nesting boxes provided by concerned birders have contributed to a promising comeback.

Year-round | Adult

WOOD THRUSH

Hylocichla mustelina L 7¾" (20 cm)

FIELD MARKS

Reddish brown above, brightest on crown and nape

White face and chest streaked and spotted in black

Rump and tail brownish olive

White eye ring

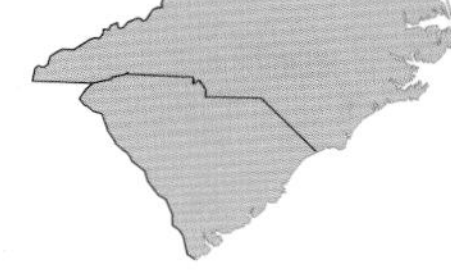

Behavior

Feeds on the ground or close to it, foraging for insects, spiders, fruits, and berries. Known to rub ants on its feathers while preening. During courtship, male chases female in quick, circling flight. Best known for its loud, liquid song of three- to five-note phrases, each usually ending with a complex trill, which can be heard in summer before daybreak or at dusk. Calls include a rapid *pit-pit-pit.*

Habitat

Common in moist, shaded undergrowth of deciduous or mixed woods, and seldom seen outside of dense forest. Dependent on this habitat, its numbers have declined since the mid-1900s.

Local Sites

This elusive bird can be found in summer in the dense undergrowth of woodlands throughout the Carolinas.

FIELD NOTES Once the Wood Thrush has left the Carolinas for its Central American wintering grounds, it is soon replaced by the similar, but slightly smaller, Hermit Thrush, *Catharus guttatus* (inset), a winter resident of dry, brushy coniferous or mixed woods. Look for its reddish brown tail and rump and the dark spotting on its breast, as well as its habit of often flicking its wings and tail.

Year-round | Adult female

AMERICAN ROBIN

Turdus migratorius L 10" (25 cm)

FIELD MARKS

Brick red underparts, paler in female and juvenile

Gray-brown above with darker head and tail

White throat and lower belly

Broken white eye ring; yellow bill

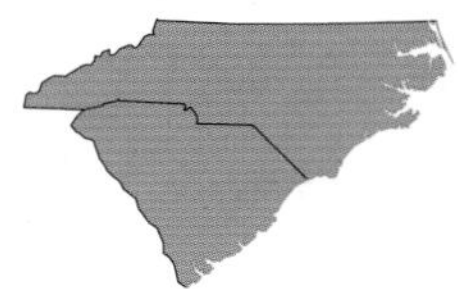

Behavior

Best known and largest of the thrushes, often seen on suburban lawns, hopping about and cocking its head in search of earthworms. The American Robin gleans butterflies, damselflies, and other flying insects from foliage and sometimes takes prey in flight. Robins also eat fruit, especially in fall and winter. This broad plant and animal diet makes them one of the most successful and wide-ranging thrushes. Calls include a rapid *tut-tut-tut;* song is a variable *cheerily cheer-up cheerio.*

Habitat

Common and widespread, the American Robin forages on lawns and nests in shrubs, trees, and even on sheltered windowsills. Winters in moist woodlands, swamps, suburbs, and parks.

Local Sites

Look for robins almost anywhere in the state, including the nearest backyard.

FIELD NOTES The juvenile robin, which can be seen every year between May and September, has a paler breast, like the female of the species, but its underparts are heavily spotted with brown. Look as well for spots of buff on its back and wings.

Year-round | Adult

GRAY CATBIRD

Dumetella carolinensis L 8½" (22 cm)

FIELD MARKS

Dark gray overall

Black cap

Long, black tail, often cocked

Undertail coverts chestnut

Dark eyes; short, dark bill

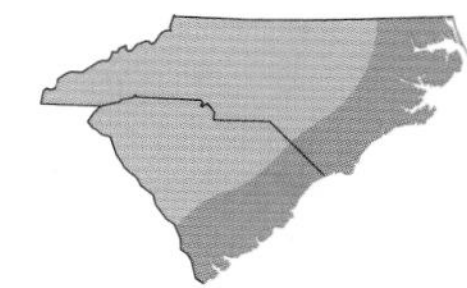

Behavior

Unless singing from an exposed perch, stays low in thick brush, foraging for insects, spiders, berries, and fruit from branches, foliage, and leaf litter. The Gray Catbird got its name from its catlike *mew* call. Song intersperses *mew* within a variable mixture of melodious, nasal, squeaky, sometimes abrasive but never repeated, notes. Jumps abruptly from one phrase to another in its rambling series of vocalizations.

Habitat

Tends to stay hidden in low, dense thickets of overgrowth in woodlands and residential areas. Female builds nest in low shrubs or in small trees with dense growth offering some protection.

Local Sites

These birds can be heard year-round at sites along the coast, or in summer throughout the Carolinas. Look for them in wooded areas, suburbs, or even city parks.

FIELD NOTES The Gray Catbird is the only mimic in the Carolinas to truly rival the Northern Mockingbird in breadth and variety of imitations. In addition to its catlike *mew*, the catbird can reproduce calls of other birds, of amphibians, even of machinery, and incorporate them into its song.

Year-round | Adult

NORTHERN MOCKINGBIRD

Mimus polyglottos L 10" (25 cm)

FIELD MARKS

Gray overall; darker above

White wing patches and outer tail feathers, which flash conspicuously in flight

Long, blackish wings and tail

Short, black bill

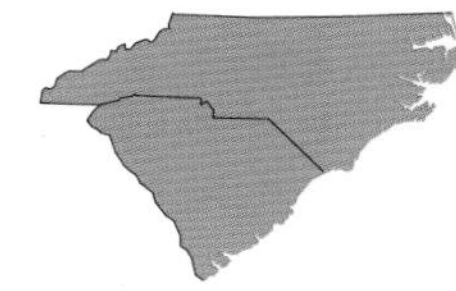

Behavior

The pugnacious Northern Mockingbird will protect its territory against other birds as well as dogs, cats, and humans. Has a varied diet that includes berries, grasshoppers, spiders, snails, and earthworms. An expert mimic, the mockingbird is known for variety of song, learning and imitating calls of many other species and animals. Typically repeats a song's phrases three times before beginning a new one. Call is a loud, sharp *check.*

Habitat

Resides in a variety of habitats, including cities, towns, and suburbs. Feeds close to the ground, in thickets or heavy vegetation.

Local Sites

The Northern Mockingbird is one of the more widespread and abundant birds throughout the Carolinas.

FIELD NOTES Though not related, the uncommon and declining Loggerhead Shrike, *Lanius ludovicianus* (inset), looks strikingly similar to the Northern Mockingbird. Note the distinguishing black mask and hooked bill of this raptorial songbird. In flight, the wings and tail are darker and the white wing patches are smaller than in the Northern Mockingbird.

Year-round | Adult

BROWN THRASHER

Toxostoma rufum L 11½" (29 cm)

FIELD MARKS

Reddish brown above

Pale buff to white below with heavy dark streaking

Long, reddish brown tail

Yellow eyes; dark, decurved bill

Two white wing bars

Behavior

Forages through leaf litter for insects, fruit, and grain; finds additional prey by digging with decurved bill. Courtship involves little fanfare, the whole process consisting of one or both birds picking up leaves or twigs and dropping them in front of the other. Sings from an exposed perch a long series of varied melodious phrases, each one given two or three times. Calls include a *smack* and a *churr.*

Habitat

Common in hedgerows, dense brush, and woodland edges. Often close to human habitation, it has adapted to living in the vegetation of suburban gardens. Nests in bushes, on ground, or in low trees.

Local Sites

Common and widespread, this distinctively streaked bird can be found in more heavily wooded areas throughout the Carolinas. Try Francis Marion and Croatan National Forests year-round, or Nantahala and Pisgah National Forests in summer.

FIELD NOTES A very creative vocalizer, the Brown Thrasher has the ability to mimic other birds, but more often sings its own song—it's got enough of them. It has been reported that the Brown Thrasher has the largest song repertoire of any North American bird; more than 1,100 types have been recorded.

Nonbreeding | Adult

EUROPEAN STARLING

Sturnus vulgaris L 8½" (22 cm)

FIELD MARKS

Iridescent black breeding plumage

Buffy tips on back, tail feathers

Fall feathers tipped in white, giving speckled appearance

Yellow bill; in summer its base is pale blue on male, pink on female

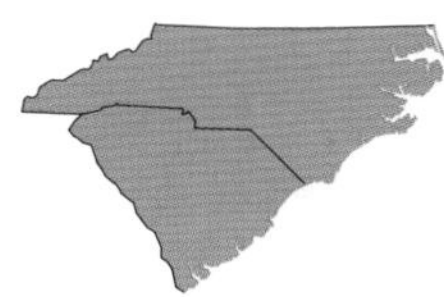

Behavior

A social and aggressive bird, the European Starling feeds on a tremendous variety of food, ranging from invertebrates—such as snails, worms, and spiders—to fruits, berries, grains, seeds, and garbage. It probes ground for food, opening its bill to create small holes. Usually seen in flocks, except during nesting season. Imitates calls of other species and emits high-pitched notes, including squeaks, hisses, chirps, and twittering.

Habitat

The adaptable starling thrives in a variety of habitats, from urban centers to agricultural regions. Nests in cavities, ranging from crevices in urban settings to woodpecker holes and nest boxes.

Local Sites

Widespread year-round throughout the Carolinas, the starling is likely to be found in most local parks.

FIELD NOTES A Eurasian species introduced into New York's Central Park in 1890, it has since spread throughout the U.S. and Canada. Abundant, bold, and aggressive, starlings often compete for and take over nest sites of other birds, including Eastern Bluebirds, Wood Ducks, Red-bellied Woodpeckers, Great Crested Flycatchers, and Purple Martins.

Year-round | Adult

CEDAR WAXWING

Bombycilla cedrorum L 7¼" (18 cm)

FIELD MARKS

Distinctive sleek crest

Black mask bordered in white

Brownish head, back, breast, and sides; pale yellow belly; gray rump

Yellow terminal tail band

May have red, waxy tips on wings

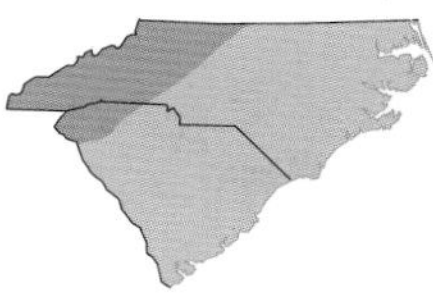

Behavior

Eats the most fruit of any bird in North America. Up to 84 percent of its diet includes cedar, peppertree, mistletoe, and hawthorn berries and crabapple fruit. Also consumes sap, flower petals, and insects. Cedar Waxwings are gregarious in nature and band together for foraging and protection. Flocks containing several to a few hundred birds may feed side by side in winter, then rapidly disperse, startling potential predators. Call is a thin, high-pitched *zeee.*

Habitat

Found in open habitats where berries are available. The abundance and location of berries influence the Cedar Waxwing's migration patterns: It moves long distances only when its food sources run out.

Local Sites

Cedar Waxwings converge in winter wherever berries and fruit are abundant.

FIELD NOTES On Appalachian breeding grounds, Cedar Waxwing pairs engage in "courtship hopping." On a shared perch, the male and female take turns hopping toward one another until they touch bills. One passes off food or another trinket such as a flower petal; the other hops away, returns, and gives it back.

Year-round | Adult male

NORTHERN PARULA

Parula americana L 4½" (11 cm)

FIELD MARKS

Throat and breast bright yellow with red patches; white belly

Gray-blue above with yellowish green upper back

Two white wing bars

Broken white orbital ring

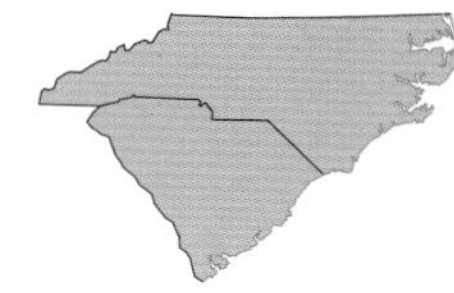

Behavior

The Carolinas' smallest warbler, the Northern Parula is a very active forager and can be observed rightside up or upside down on tree trunks seeking out larvae, hovering in search of caterpillars or spiders, or in aerial pursuit of flying insects. Song can be heard from the treetops during nesting or migration, consisting of a rising, buzz-like trill, ending in an abrupt *zip*.

Habitat

Common in coniferous or mixed woods, especially near water. Prefers to nest in trees covered either with the lichen *Usnea* or Spanish moss.

Local Sites

To find a nesting Parula, look for the pale green, stringy *Usnea* lichen or Spanish moss hanging from branches of trees in Congaree National Park, Francis Beidler Forest, or throughout the Appalachian Mountains.

FIELD NOTES The Northern Parula is quite picky when it comes to its nesting materials. If it cannot find a tree covered in *Usnea* lichen or Spanish moss, it will fly as far as a mile away to secure a single piece for use as padding. A decrease in the amount of this lichen on the Atlantic coast due to air pollution is currently threatening the warbler's population in the Carolinas.

Immature | "Myrtle"

YELLOW-RUMPED WARBLER

Dendroica coronata L 5½" (14 cm)

FIELD MARKS

Bright yellow rump; yellow patch on sides of breast; pale eyebrow; white throat and sides of neck

Winter birds grayish brown above, white below with brown streaking

Breeding birds have yellow patch on crown, grayish blue upperparts

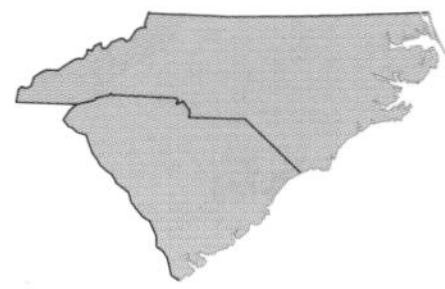

Behavior

The most abundant winter warbler in the Carolinas, it darts about branches from tree to tree or in bushes, foraging for myrtle berries and seeds. Often seen in winter in small foraging flocks. Will switch to primarily insect diet before spring migration. Songs of the eastern subspecies, the "Myrtle Warbler," include a slow warble and a musical trill. Call is a low, flat *check*.

Habitat

Common in fall and winter in brushy and wooded habitats, especially at field edges and on barrier islands. Seeks out areas rich in bayberry or juniper thickets.

Local Sites

Winter residents throughout much of the Carolinas, Yellow-rumped Warblers are abundant along the Carolinas' coast during fall migration. Look for them in the thickets of Fort Fisher State Recreation Area.

FIELD NOTES While these birds are preparing to leave for northerly breeding grounds around April, look for the male's bright breeding plumage (inset), characterized by a yellow crown patch and grayish blue upperparts. The female has a smaller crown patch and dusky brown upperparts.

Year-round | Adult male

PINE WARBLER

Dendroica pinus L 5½" (14 cm)

FIELD MARKS

Yellow throat color extends onto sides of neck and breast

Male is greenish olive above with dark streaks on sides of breast

Female is duller overall

Belly and undertail coverts white

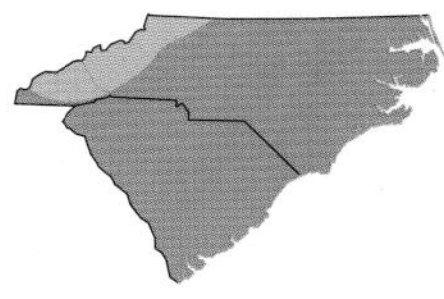

Behavior

Forages high up in pine trees, methodically gleaning insects, caterpillars, and spiders from bark and needles, but will also feed on ground and along lower branches for insects, seeds, grapes, and berries. Also makes aerial dives at flying insects. Though territorially aggressive in breeding season toward other species sharing the same stand of pines, in winter the Pine Warbler may feed in mixed flocks with bluebirds and Yellow-rumped Warblers. A very vocal bird, its song is a musical trill, varying in speed. Call is a slurred *tsup.*

Habitat

Favors open stands of pines, especially while breeding; conceals nest among the needles at branch tips. Winters in pines and mixed woodlands.

Local Sites

The Pine Warbler can be found year-round high up in the trees of Santee National Wildlife Refuge.

FIELD NOTES The Pine Warbler and Common Yellowthroat are the only two members of their large family that are found year-round in the Carolinas. The winter yellowthroats though are most likely not the same ones you see in summer. The Pine Warbler on the other hand tends to remain near its breeding grounds all year.

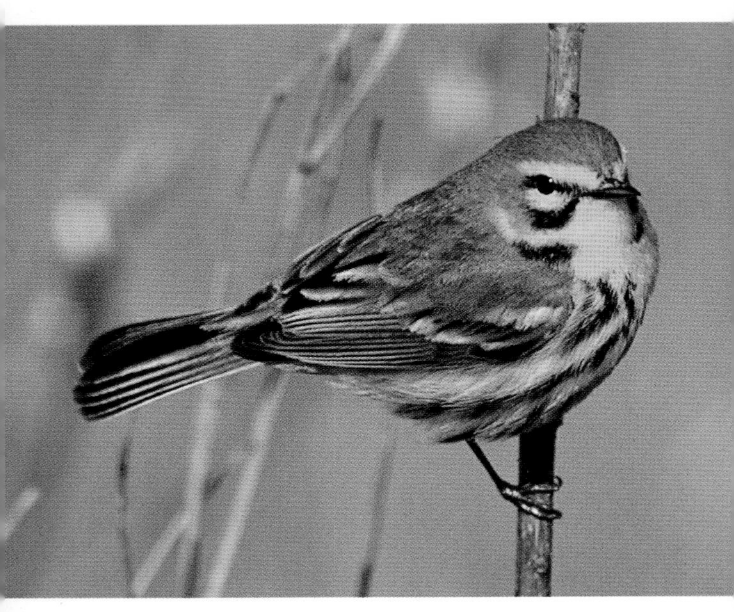

Year-round | Adult male

PRAIRIE WARBLER

Dendroica discolor L 4¾" (12 cm)

FIELD MARKS

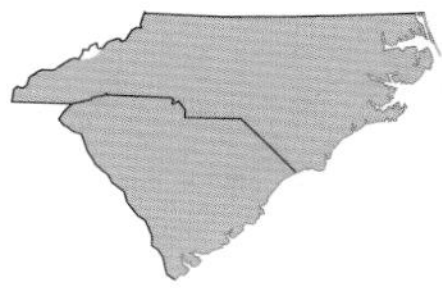

Bright yellow below with black streaks on sides

Olive above; faint chestnut streaks on back, more visible on male

Bright yellow above and below eye; black line through and below eyes on male

Behavior

A very active bird, it constantly pumps its tail while foraging for insects and spiders on bushes, low tree branches, or the ground. Generally solitary or in a pair, but joins mixed flocks on migration. Sings from exposed perch its distinctive song, a rising series of buzzy *zee* notes. Call is a rich, full *chick.*

Habitat

Open second-growth woodlands, especially ones with pines, scrublands, and overgrown fields, but not prairies (it was misnamed when first found). Cup-shaped nest is hidden in trees or bushes.

Local Sites

The Prairie Warbler is partial to dune woodlands and open stands of pine. Look for it in summer in wooded areas of the coast or inland at Carolina Sandhills National Wildlife Refuge.

FIELD NOTES A frequent host of the Brown-headed Cowbird's nest parasitism, the Prairie Warbler is becoming even more vulnerable as its habitat is further restricted by ongoing development. Since it raises only two broods each year, even if one is jeopardized by the cowbird's egg-dropping, the future of this species may depend upon careful land management.

Breeding | Adult male

BLACK-AND-WHITE WARBLER

Mniotilta varia L 5½" (13 cm)

FIELD MARK

Boldly striped black-and-white on head, body, and undertail coverts

Male's throat and cheeks are black; in winter, chin is white

Females and immatures have white cheeks and throats

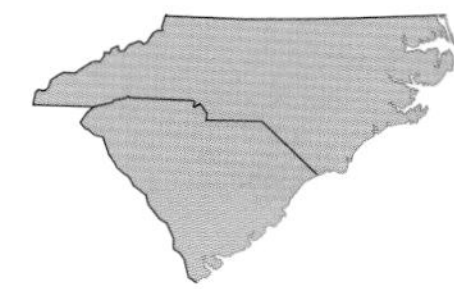

Behavior

Creeps around branches and up and down tree trunks, foraging like a nuthatch or creeper, though it does not use its tail to prop up its body. Probes crevices in the bark of trees with its long bill for insects, caterpillars, and spiders. If disturbed at nest, female drags wings on the ground with tail spread for distraction. Song is a series of high, thin *wee-see* notes; calls include a sharp *chip* and a high *seep-seep.*

Habitat

Prefers woodlands, both deciduous and mixed, as well as forested margins of swamps and rivers. Nests on the ground or in the hollow of a stump or log.

Local Sites

The Black-and-white Warbler breeds commonly in the woods around Walhalla State Fish Hatchery.

FIELD NOTES The only other warbler with a foraging style similar to the Black-and-white's is the less common Yellow-throated Warbler, *Dendroica dominica* (inset). In summer, it inhabits many of the same stretches of mature woods as the Black-and-white, but tends to forage higher up. Look for its bright yellow chin and throat, its black face, and its white eyebrow.

Year-round | Adult male

AMERICAN REDSTART

Setophaga ruticilla L 5¼" (13 cm)

FIELD MARKS

Male is glossy black above and on hood; bright orange patches on sides, wings, and tail

Female gray-olive above; orange patches replaced with yellow

White belly and undertail coverts

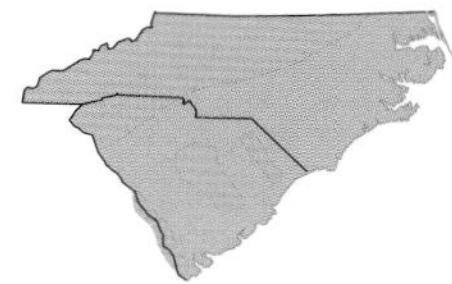

Behavior

Often fans its tail and spreads its wings when perched. Darts suddenly to snare flying insects. Also takes insects, caterpillars, spiders, berries, fruit, and seeds from branches and foliage. Broad, flattened bill, ringed by bristles, is well suited for flycatching as well as gleaning. Sings often, a series of high, thin notes usually followed by a single, wheezy, downslurred note. Call is a thin, squeaky *chip*.

Habitat

Common in moist deciduous and mixed woodlands with thick undergrowth, also in riparian and second-growth woodlands. Nests in forks of trees or bushes generally 10 to 20 feet from the ground.

Local Sites

Redstarts are most evident in summer in the woodlands of the Appalachians, such as those found in Great Smoky Mountains National Park.

FIELD NOTES An immature male resembles a female. By his first spring, he has gained black lores and some black spotting on the breast, but his wing and tail patches are still a dull orange-yellow. A year-old male trying to breed in this plumage is at a great disadvantage. It is not until his second fall that he acquires full adult plumage and is attractive to females.

Year-round | Adult male

PROTHONOTARY WARBLER

Protonotaria citrea L 5½" (14 cm)

FIELD MARKS

Male's head and underparts golden yellow; female duller

Blue-gray wings

Blue-gray tail has white patches; white undertail coverts

Large dark eyes; long black bill

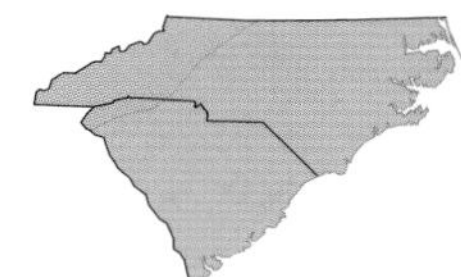

Behavior

Deliberate in plucking insects, larvae, spiders, and seeds from crevices in ground, logs, and trees. Also picks snails and crustaceans right out of water. After arriving on breeding grounds and building several partial nests, male sings incessantly until female arrives and chooses a nest to complete. Song is a series of loud, ringing *zweet* notes; call is a dry *chip*.

Habitat

Common in moist lowland forests, woodlands prone to flooding, and stream banks, but wanders far during migration. Unlike most warblers, nests in tree cavities, nest boxes, or similar crannies, always near water.

Local Sites

Francis Beidler Forest and Alligator River National Wildlife Refuge provide the specific habitat niche these warblers require to nest.

FIELD NOTES The Yellow Warbler, *Dendroica petechia* (inset), shares with the Prothonotary a prominent dark eye, a bright yellow face, and a preference for wet habitats. In the Carolinas, it nests primarily in the Appalachians. The male (inset, top) has conspicuous red streaks on his breast.

Year-round | Adult

LOUISIANA WATERTHRUSH

Seiurus motacilla L 6" (15 cm)

FIELD MARKS

White underparts with dark streaking; salmon-buff flanks

Olive-brown above and on crown

Eyebrow is pale buff in front of eye, whiter and broader behind

White, unstreaked chin and throat

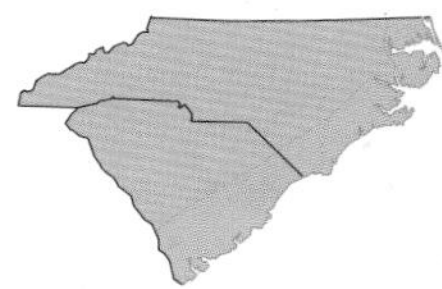

Behavior

The Louisiana Waterthrush bobs its tail to the side, slowly but constantly, as it forages on the ground, walking rather than hopping. Feeds on aquatic and terrestrial insects, mollusks, and small fish along stream banks or in shallows. Sings from an exposed perch or on the ground a clear, musical song which begins with three or four downslurred *sew* notes, followed by a brief, rapid jumble. Call is a sharp *chink*.

Habitat

Found near mountain streams in dense woodlands, also in wooded floodplains and swamps. Nests under roots or in crevices in riparian areas.

Local Sites

The streams and ponds of Walhalla State Fish Hatchery in Sumter National Forest host nesting Louisiana Waterthrushes every summer. They can also be found at sites throughout the Appalachian Mountains.

FIELD NOTES The Louisiana Waterthrush is one of the earliest warblers to arrive in the Carolinas every spring. It quickly begins establishing its territory, which invariably runs along a fairly straight line—along the course of the stream on which it will raise its young.

Year-round | Adult male

COMMON YELLOWTHROAT

Geothlypis trichas L 5" (13 cm)

FIELD MARKS

Adult male shows broad, black mask bordered above by light gray

Female lacks black mask, has whitish patch around its eyes

Grayish olive upperparts; bright yellow throat and breast; yellow undertail coverts

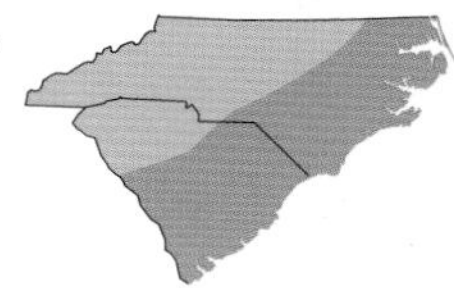

Behavior

This widespread warbler generally remains close to ground, skulking and hiding in undergrowth. May also be seen climbing vertically on stems. While foraging, cocks tail and hops on ground to glean insects, caterpillars, and spiders from foliage, twigs, and reeds. Sometimes feeds while hovering, or gives chase to flying insects. One version of variable song is a loud, rolling *wichity-wichity-wich.* Calls include a raspy *chuck.*

Habitat

Stays low in marshes, shrubby fields, woodland edges, and thickets near water. Nests atop piles of weeds and grass, or in small shrubs.

Local Sites

Yellowthroats are found year-round on the Carolinas' coastal plain from Savannah to Alligator River National Wildlife Refuges.

FIELD NOTES The largest North American warbler at 7½", the Yellow-breasted Chat, *Icteria virens* (inset), is also one of the most elusive. Like the yellowthroat, it remains low to the ground, hidden in dense vegetation. Listen for its harsh, jumbled, unmusical song, given from a perch or in flight.

Year-round | Adult male

SUMMER TANAGER

Piranga rubra L 7¾" (20 cm)

FIELD MARKS

Adult male is rosy red overall

Most females have olive green upperparts, yellow underparts

Some females have overall reddish wash

Large yellowish bill; slight crest

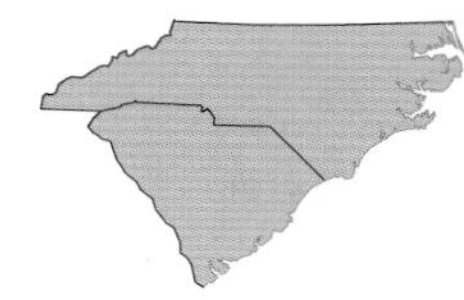

Behavior

With the largest range of any North American tanager, the Summer Tanager nests throughout the Carolinas. Snags bees and wasps in midair, sometimes even raiding their hives. After catching one, the Summer Tanager brings the bee back to its perch, then beats it against a branch and wipes the body along bark to remove the stinger before eating. In addition, deliberately and methodically picks insects, caterpillars, and fruit from leaves. Melodic, warbling song is robin-like. Call is a staccato *ki-ti-tuk*.

Habitat

Stays high up in trees of deciduous and mixed forests, especially ones rich in pines and oaks. Female builds nest far up and out on limbs of trees.

Local Sites

In summer look high up in the trees of Francis Marion, Croatan, or Pisgah National Forests for this bird's brilliant red plumage.

FIELD NOTES The Scarlet Tanager, *Piranga olivacea* (inset), commonly breeds in deciduous forests in Appalachian regions of the Carolinas. Like the Summer Tanager, the male has a bright red body, but is set apart by his black wings and tail. The female Scarlet is olive above and yellow below with darker wings and tail.

Year-round | Adult female

EASTERN TOWHEE

Pipilo erythrophthalmus L 7½" (19 cm)

FIELD MARKS

Male has black hood, upperparts

Female similarly patterned, but black areas replaced by brown

Rufous sides; white underparts

White corners on long tail

Red or straw-colored eyes

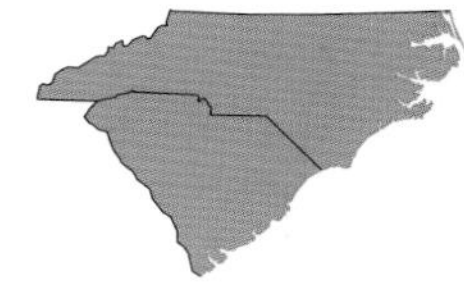

Behavior

Stays low to ground, scratching it frequently with feet together, head held low, and tail up, exposing seeds and insects, such as beetles and caterpillars, on which it feeds. Also forages for grasshoppers, spiders, moths, and fruit. Known to sing from an exposed perch, *drink your tea*, sometimes shortened to *drink tea*; though songs vary with each bird. Also calls in a clear, slightly upslurred *swee*. On North Carolina's Outer Banks, listen for birds who give a raspy *mer* call.

Habitat

Prefers partial to second-growth woodlands, with dense shrubs, brushy thickets, and extensive leaf litter. Also seen in brambly fields, hedgerows, riparian areas, and forest clearings. Nests on the ground, near shrubs.

Local Sites

Listen for these birds scratching the leaf litter of wooded areas throughout the Carolinas year-round.

FIELD NOTES The male Eastern Towhee (inset) is similarly patterned as the female, but with brown areas replaced by black. It also has more distinct white patches on its primary and tertial wing feathers, which it displays during courtship by fanning its wings.

Breeding | Adult

CHIPPING SPARROW

Spizella passerina L 5½" (14 cm)

FIELD MARKS

Breeding adult shows bright chestnut crown, white eyebrow, gray cheek and nape

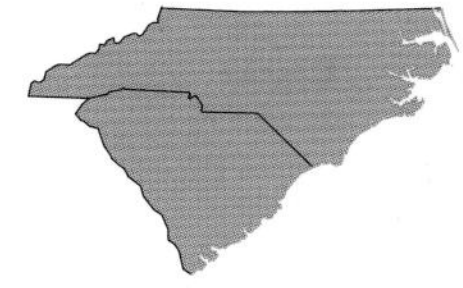

Winter adult has streaked brown crown and a brown face

Streaked brown wings and back, unstreaked gray breast and belly

Behavior

Forages on the ground for insects, caterpillars, spiders, and seeds. May be found foraging in small family flocks in fall or in mixed-species groups in winter. Sings from high perch a one-pitched, rapid-fire trill of dry *chip* notes. Call in flight or when foraging is a high, hard *seep* or *tsik*.

Habitat

The Chipping Sparrow can be found in suburban lawns and gardens, woodland edges, and pine-oak forests. Tends to more open areas in winter. Nests close to the ground in branches or vine tangles.

Local Sites

Found year-round throughout the Carolinas, the Chipping Sparrow could be encountered in any of the region's protected areas, such as Weymouth Woods or Webb Wildlife Center, or in the nearest backyard.

FIELD NOTES Once breeding season is through, the Chipping Sparrow will turn to a primarily seed diet. Like the Field Sparrow, it employs the clever strategy of landing atop a reed so as to bend it by the force of its weight, in the process dislodging the seeds within.

Year-round | Adult

FIELD SPARROW

Spizella pusilla L 5¾" (15 cm)

FIELD MARKS

Gray face with rufous crown; some with rufous behind eyes

Distinct white eye ring; pink bill

Streaked brown back and wings

Breast and sides gray or buff-colored; belly grayish white

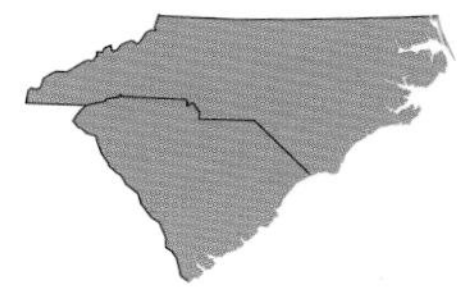

Behavior

Remains low to the ground in fields and open brush, foraging for insects, caterpillars, seeds, and spiders. Seen in small family groups after breeding and in larger, mixed-species foraging flocks in winter. Song is a series of clear, flute-like whistles accelerating into a trill; call note is a harsh *chip*. In flight, listen for a clear, descending *tsew*.

Habitat

Found commonly in open, brushy woodlands and fields. Female builds nest on the ground or in a bush low to the ground, often near water.

Local Sites

Though its habitat is becoming more restricted in the Carolinas, the Field Sparrow is still liable to be found year-round throughout the region. Look for it in the open woodlands around Hartwell Lake as well as in Santee, Alligator River, and Mattamuskeet National Wildlife Refuges.

FIELD NOTES Field Sparrows flourished with the widespread clearing of eastern woodlands in the 1900s, which opened up countless acres of ideal nesting habitat for this bird. Now that suburbs are taking over farmlots across the eastern seaboard, their numbers are being whittled back down.

Year-round | Adult

SAVANNAH SPARROW

Passerculus sandwichensis L 5½" (14 cm)

FIELD MARKS

Yellow or whitish eyebrow

Pale median crown stripe on streaked crown

Dark brown streaked upperparts

White below with brown streaking on chin, breast, and flanks

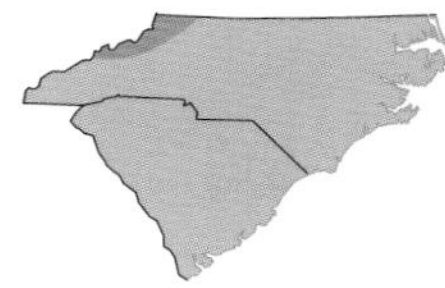

Behavior

Seen regularly in small, loose flocks, foraging on the ground for seeds and berries in the fall and winter, sometimes scratching like a towhee. Roosts on the ground. When alarmed, often runs through grasses on the ground instead of flying. Song begins with two or three *chip* notes, then two buzzy trills. Flight call is a thin *seep.*

Habitat

Common in a variety of open habitats: marshes, farm fields, grasslands, golf courses, and grassy dunes.

Local Sites

Savannah Sparrows are winter residents of open areas at sites such as Hartwell Lake and Santee National Wildlife Refuge. Look as well for the larger, paler "Ipswich" subspecies on coastal dunes like those at Huntington Beach State Park and Fort Fisher State Recreation Area.

FIELD NOTES Another of the Carolinas' strictly winter sparrows, the larger and less common Fox Sparrow, *Passerella iliaca* (inset), can at first glance be confused with the Savannah. It is much more rufous overall though, and its breast streaking converges into a large central splotch. Like the Savannah, it remains close to the ground, foraging like a towhee, but it tends to more densely wooded areas.

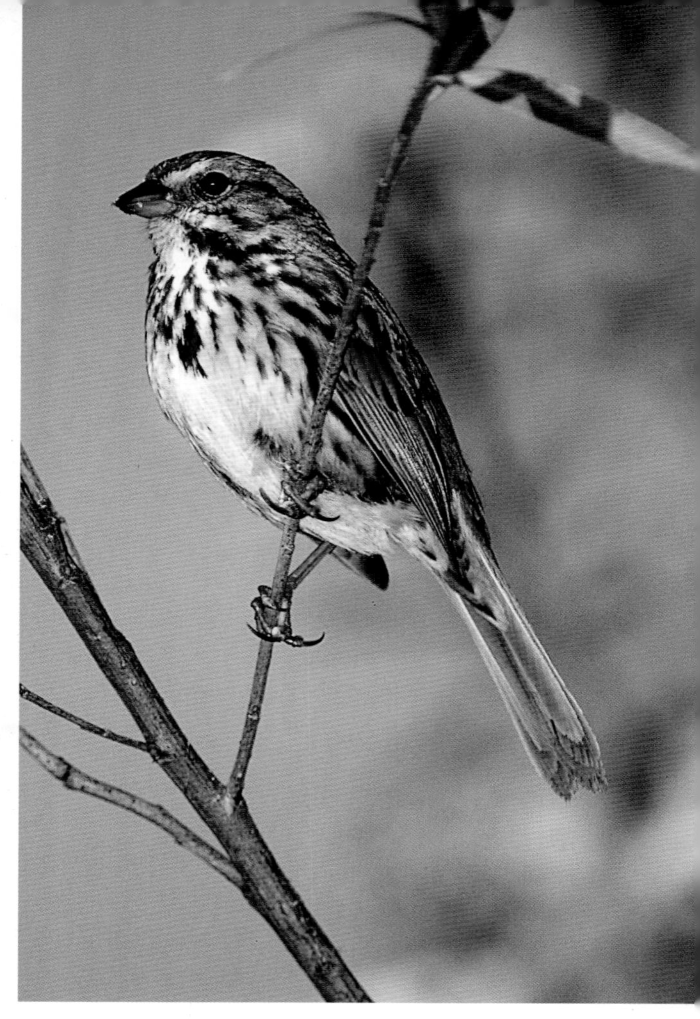

Year-round | Adult

SONG SPARROW

Melospiza melodia L 5¾" (16 cm)

FIELD MARKS

Underparts whitish, with streaks on sides and breast that converge into a dark breast spot

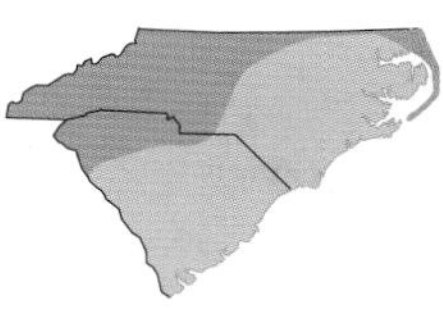

Streaked brown and gray above; broad, grayish eyebrow; broad, dark malar stripe

Rounded tail

Behavior

Forages in trees and bushes and on ground for larvae, fruits, and berries, sometimes scratching ground to unearth grain or insects. Coastal birds take mollusks and crustaceans as well. Female broods young while male defends territory intently, singing from exposed perch and battling competitors. Perches in the open, belting out its melodious song, three to four short, clear notes followed by a buzzy *tow-wee* and a trill.

Habitat

Common in suburban and rural gardens, weedy fields, dense streamside thickets, and forest edges. Nests on the ground or near it in trees and bushes.

Local Sites

A common species in winter throughout the Carolinas. Listen for the Song Sparrow's melodious song year-round in the Outer Banks.

FIELD NOTES The Swamp Sparrow, *Melospiza georgiana* (inset), tends to remain in wetter areas than its more heavily streaked cousin, the Song Sparrow. A winter visitor to the Carolinas, it sometimes forages by wading into water and picking organisms off the surface. Look for its rufous and gray crown, its reddish brown wings, and the blurry streaks on its grayish breast.

Year-round | Adult

WHITE-THROATED SPARROW

Zonotrichia albicollis L 6¾" (17 cm)

FIELD MARKS

Broad eyebrow is yellow in front of eye, white or tan behind

Black crown stripes and eye lines

White throat bordered by gray

Streaked rusty brown above, grayish below

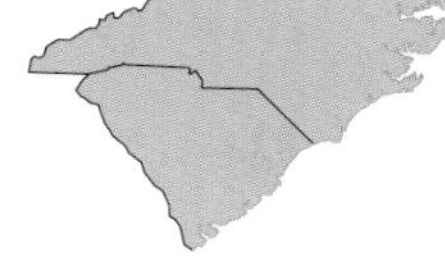

Behavior

Almost always seen in a flock in winter, employs the double-scratch foraging method of towhees; that is, it rakes leaf litter with a backward kick of both feet, keeping its head held low and its tail pointed up. Also forages in bushes and trees for seeds, fruit, tree buds, and insects. Often heard before seen, its calls include a sharp *pink* and a drawn out, lisping *tseep*. Its song, sung year-round, is a slow, thin whistle consisting of two single notes then three triple notes: *pure-sweet-Canada-Canada-Canada.*

Habitat

Common winterer in woodland undergrowth, forest edges, and gardens; frequently seen at platform feeders.

Local Sites

Found in thickets throughout the Carolinas in winter, look for this bird's distinctive head pattern at Francis Marion and Croatan National Forests, at Alligator River and Santee National Wildlife Refuges, around Hartwell Lake, and into the Appalachians.

FIELD NOTES Winter flocks double-scratching in dense undergrowth can be detected audibly if you keep your ears open, but getting a good view of this species can be more difficult. Try producing a *pish* sound yourself, a technique which can often bring the bird right to you.

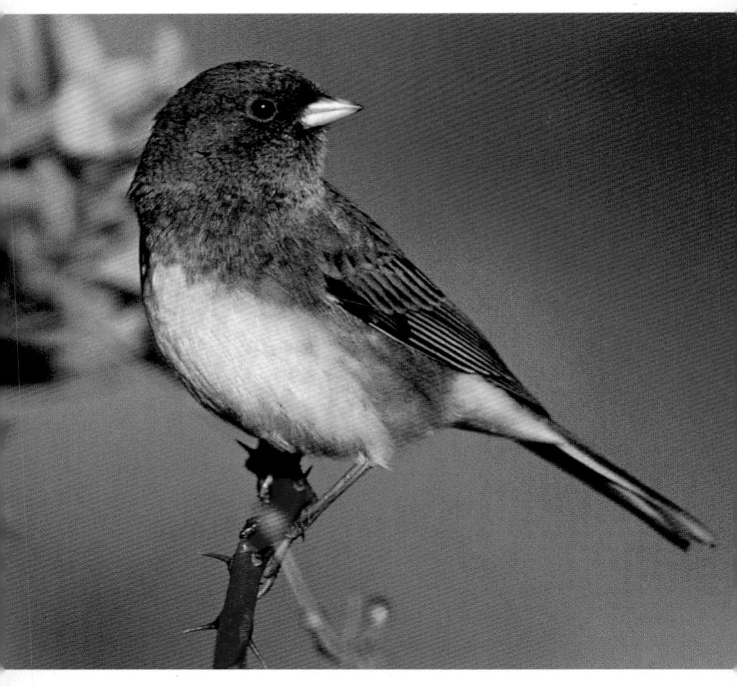

Year-round | Adult male "Slate-colored"

DARK-EYED JUNCO

Junco hyemalis L 6¼" (16 cm)

FIELD MARKS

Dark gray hood and upperparts on male, brownish on female

White outer tail feathers in flight

White belly and undertail coverts

Pale pinkish bill

Juvenile streaked brown overall

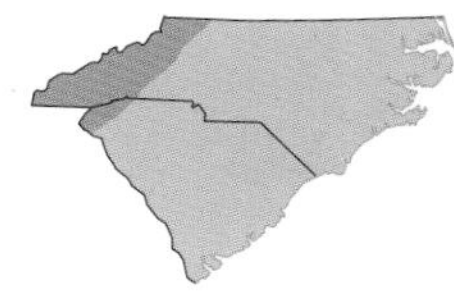

Behavior

Scratches on ground and forages by gleaning seeds, grain, berries, insects, caterpillars, and fruit from plants. Will occasionally give chase to a flying insect. Forms flocks in winter, when males may remain farther north or at greater elevations than immatures and females. Song is a short, musical trill that varies in pitch and tempo. Calls include a sharp *dit,* and a rapid twittering in flight.

Habitat

Winters in a wide variety of habitats, especially patchy wooded areas. Breeds in coniferous or mixed woodlands of the Appalachians. Nests on or close to ground, sheltered by a bush or in a cavity such as a tree root.

Local Sites

Flocks of these small sparrows are abundant and conspicuous in winter in wooded areas and at feeders throughout the Carolinas. Look for them year-round in the Appalachians and at nearby sites such as Caesars Head State Park and Table Rock State Park.

FIELD NOTES The various subspecies of the Dark-eyed Junco were unified into one species in 1973, although they are widely scattered geographically and fairly disparate in their field marks. They do have in common white outer tail feathers, behavioral habits, and, most significantly, genetic makeup.

Year-round | Adult male

NORTHERN CARDINAL

Cardinalis cardinalis L 8¾" (22 cm)

FIELD MARKS

Male is red overall, black face

Female is buffy brown tinged with red on wings, crest, and tail

Large, conspicuous crest

Cone-shaped, reddish bill; blackish on juvenile

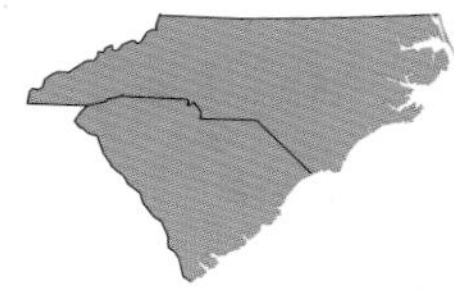

Behavior

The state bird of North Carolina, generally seen alone or in a pair in summer, in small groups in winter. Forages on the ground or low in shrubs mainly for insects, seeds, leaf buds, berries, and fruit. A non-migratory songbird, the Cardinal has adapted so well to landscaped yards and backyard feeders that it continues to expand its range northward into Canada. Sings a variety of melodious songs year-round, including a *cue cue-cue*, a *cheer-cheer-cheer*, and a *purty-purty-purty*. Listen for courtship duets in spring.

Habitat

Year-round resident in gardens and parks, woodland edges, streamside thickets, and practically any environment that provides thick, brushy cover. Nests in forks of trees and bushes, or in tangles of twigs and vines.

Local Sites

Cardinals are year-round residents throughout the Carolinas in woods, thickets, and parks. A hardy species, they do not shy away from areas of human habitation, and can be found even in cities.

FIELD NOTES Aggressive in defending its territory, a Cardinal will attack not only other birds, but also itself, reflected in windows, rear-view mirrors, chrome surfaces, and hubcaps.

Year-round | Adult male

BLUE GROSBEAK

Passerina caerulea L 6¾" (17 cm)

FIELD MARKS

Adult male deep blue overall with black face and wide chestnut wing bars

Female dull brownish overall

Large, heavy bill; upper mandible darker than lower

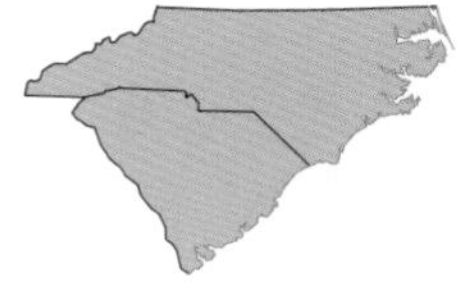

Behavior

Groups of birds arrive in spring, but soon after disperse into pairs. Forages by hopping around on the ground for insects, snails, fruit, grain, and seeds. Will fly from perch to hawk insects in mid-air, and occasionally hovers to glean insects from leaves and twigs. Has a habit of twitching and spreading its tail. Distinctive call is a loud *chink*. Song is a full-bodied series of rising and falling warbles.

Habitat

Any low, brushy habitat along a stream, golf course, marsh, roadway, or woodland edge, especially one near water. Nests low in trees, bushes, or clumps of weeds.

Local Sites

Blue Grosbeaks prefer wooded wetlands for their nesting. Look for them in summer in Francis Marion and Croatan National Forests, or at Santee and Mattamuskeet National Wildlife Refuges.

FIELD NOTES The Blue Grosbeak's cousin, the Rose-breasted Grosbeak, *Pheucticus ludovicianus* (inset, male), can be found in summer breeding in the Appalachians, or in fall migrating through the whole of the Carolinas. Look for the male's rose-red breast on otherwise black-and-white plumage.

Breeding | Adult male

INDIGO BUNTING

Passerina cyanea L 5½" (14 cm)

FIELD MARKS

Breeding male deep blue overall, darker on head; blackish wings

Female is brownish, with diffuse streaking on breast and flanks and a bluish tail

Fall male has varied amount of brown on back, breast, and lores

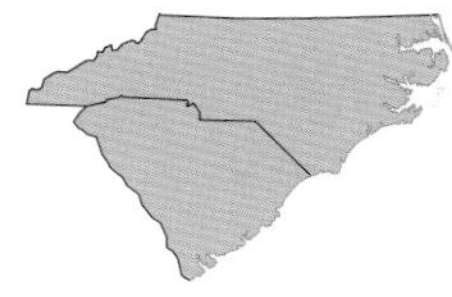

Behavior

Forages alone or in pairs for insects from ground level to canopy in spring and summer, switching to a mainly seed and berry diet in the fall. Uses its heavy conical bill to crack or hull seeds. Sings a series of varied phrases, usually doubled, *sweet-sweet* or *here-here,* often ending with a trill. Second-year males appear to learn songs from competing males, rather than from parents.

Habitat

Prefers edges and bushy transition zones between old fields and woodlands. Range is the greatest of all buntings, extending northward to southern Canada. Nests in dense shrubs and low trees.

Local Sites

Summer visitors across the Carolinas, Indigo Buntings frequent the National Forests of the Carolinas, as well as sites such as Weymouth Woods and Hartwell Lake.

FIELD NOTES The female Indigo Bunting (inset) with her brown back, buffy wing bars, and slightly streaked undersides tends to resemble a sparrow if seen alone. Look for her bluish tail, bicolored bill, and unstreaked head and back to tell her apart.

Year-round | Adult male

PAINTED BUNTING

Passerina ciris L 5½" (14 cm)

FIELD MARKS

Adult male has purplish blue head; red eye ring, breast, and rump; bright green back

Female is bright green above, paler yellow-green below

Juvenile resembles female, but duller overall

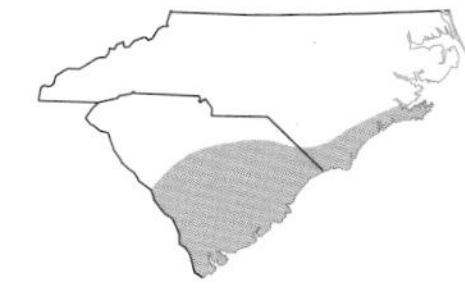

Behavior

Forages alone or in a pair, hopping on ground or low in trees and shrubs for insects, caterpillars, and seeds. Males are feisty and may draw blood—or even fight to the death—to defend territory. Courtship display consists of male spreading wings and tail, puffing up body feathers, and performing before female in a herky-jerky motion. Female carries out work of nest-building and incubation. Male sings from exposed perch a high-pitched, musical warble; call is a loud, rich *chip.*

Habitat

Locally common in streamside thickets and moist, brushy lowlands. Nests close to ground in dense foliage of bush, tree, or vine tangle.

Local Sites

A breeder along the coast south from Cedar Island National Wildlife Refuge, the Painted Bunting can be found in summer at sites like Webb Wildlife Center, ACE Basin and Cape Romain National Wildlife Refuges, and Fort Fisher State Recreation Area.

FIELD NOTES Declining in the Carolinas as its habitat is further given over to development, the Painted Bunting is fighting another battle on its wintering grounds in Mexico, where it is one of the most widely trapped and traded species due to the male's brightly colored plumage and melodious song.

Year-round | Adult male

RED-WINGED BLACKBIRD

Agelaius phoeniceus L 8¾" (22 cm)

FIELD MARKS

Male is glossy black with bright red shoulder patches broadly edged in buffy yellow

Females densely streaked overall

Pointed black bill

Wings slightly rounded at tips

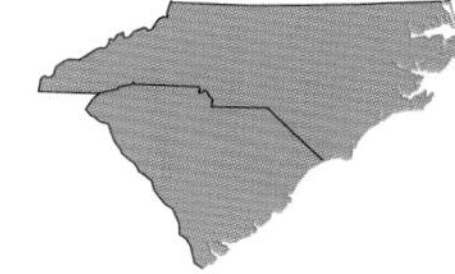

Behavior

Forages for insects, seeds, and grains in pastures and open fields. The male's bright red shoulder patches are usually visible when it sings from a perch, often atop a cattail or tall weed stalk, defending its territory. At other times only the yellow border may be visible. Territorially aggressive, a male's social status is dependent on the amount of red he displays on his shoulders. Song is a liquid, gurgling *konk-la-reee,* ending in a trill. Call is a low *chack* note.

Habitat

Breeds in colonies, mainly in freshwater marshes and wet fields with thick vegetation. Nests in cattails, bushes, or dense grass near water. During winter, flocks forage in wooded swamps and farm fields.

Local Sites

The Red-winged is common year-round in wetlands throughout the Carolinas.

FIELD NOTES Though usually much less visible within large flocks of singing males, the female Red-winged (inset) is characterized by dark brown, streaked upperparts and dusky white underparts heavily streaked with dark brown. In winter you may find a whole flock of just females.

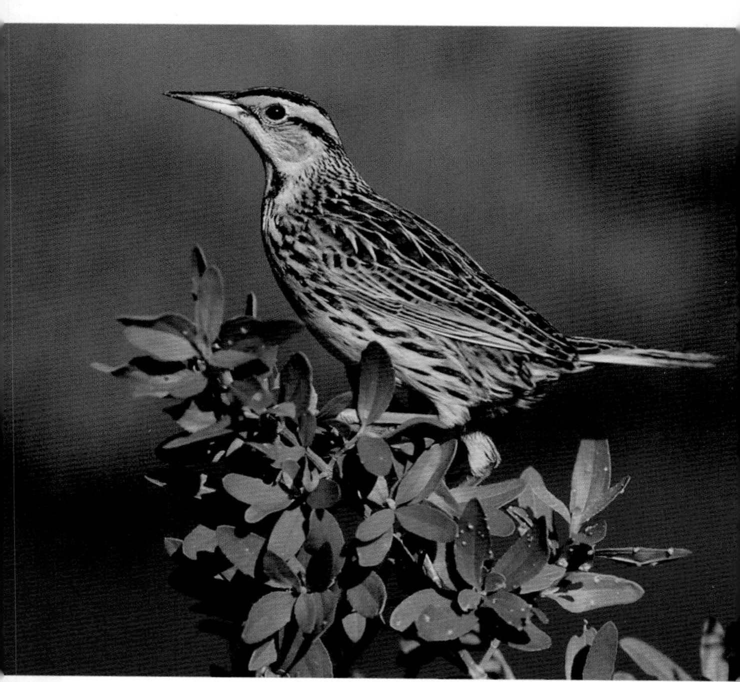

Breeding | Adult

EASTERN MEADOWLARK

Sturnella magna L 9½" (24 cm)

FIELD MARKS

Yellow below, with black V-shaped breast band, paler in winter

Black-and-white striped crown with yellow supraloral area

Brown above streaked with black

White outer tail feathers

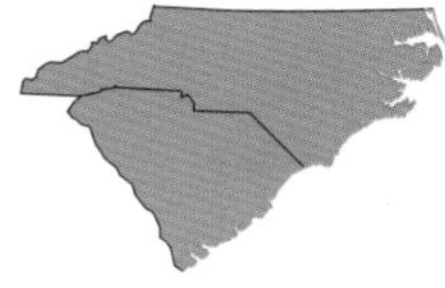

Behavior

Flicks its tail open and shut while foraging on the ground, feeding mainly on insects during spring and summer, seeds and agricultural grain in late fall and winter. Generally solitary in summer, the Meadowlark forms small flocks in fall and winter. Male known to brood while female starts second nest. Often perches on fence posts or telephone poles to sing a clear, whistled *see-you see-yeeer.* Flight call is a buzzy *drzzt.*

Habitat

Prefers the open space offered by grasslands, pastures, meadows, and farm fields. Female constructs a domed nest on the ground that is often woven into the surrounding live grasses.

Local Sites

Areas of enough open space to host the Eastern Meadowlark can be found at Santee National Wildlife Refuge, Hartwell Lake, Huntington Beach State Park, and Fort Fisher State Recreation Area.

FIELD NOTES Though its breeding range has been advancing northward due to the widespread clearing of forests, the Eastern Meadowlark population has been slowly declining in the eastern states during the past few decades as it loses suitable habitat to suburban sprawl.

Year-round | Adult male

COMMON GRACKLE

Quiscalus quiscula L 12½" (32 cm)

FIELD MARKS

Plumage appears all black; in good light, male shows glossy purplish hood, green back

Long, wedge-shaped tail

Pale yellow eyes

Narrow, pointed beak

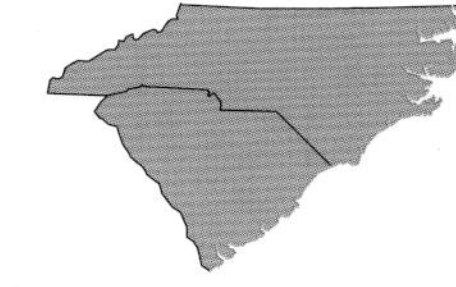

Behavior

Usually seen in a flock, this grackle moves to large, noisy, communal roosts in the evening. During the day, mainly seen on the ground in a group, feeding on insects, spiders, grubs, and earthworms. Also wades into shallow water to forage for minnows and crayfish. Known to feast on eggs and baby birds. Courtship display consists of male puffing out shoulder feathers to make a collar, drooping his wings, and singing. These birds produce sounds like ripping cloth or cracking twigs. Call note is a loud *chuck*.

Habitat

Prefers open spaces provided by farm fields, pastures, marshes, and suburban yards. Requires wooded areas, especially conifers, for nesting and roosting.

Local Sites

Common Grackles are abundant and gregarious year-round throughout the Carolinas.

FIELD NOTES The closely related Boat-tailed Grackle, *Quiscalus major* (inset), a resident of coastal salt marshes, is larger than the Common Grackle and has duller, brownish eyes. Look for its long, keel-shaped tail all along the Carolinas' coast.

Year-round | Adult male

BROWN-HEADED COWBIRD

Molothrus ater L 7½" (19 cm)

FIELD MARKS

Male's brown head contrasts with metallic black body

Female gray-brown above, paler below with a whitish throat

Short, dark, pointed bill

Juveniles streaked below

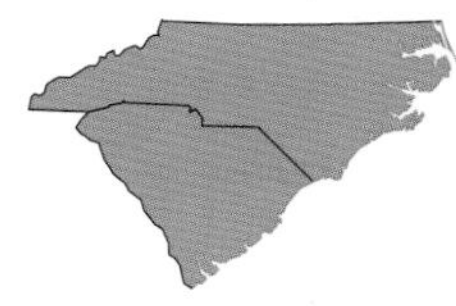

Behavior

Often forages on the ground among herds of cattle, feeding on insects flushed by the grazing farm animals. Also feeds heavily on grass seeds and agricultural grain, and is sometimes viewed as a threat to crops. Generally cocks its tail up while feeding. The Brown-headed Cowbird is a nest parasite and lays its eggs in the nests of other species, leaving the responsibilities of feeding and fledging of young to the host birds. Song is a squeaky gurgling. Calls includes a squeaky whistle.

Habitat

Cowbirds prefer open habitat such as farmlands, pastures, prairies, and edgelands bordering forests. Also found in general around human habitation.

Local Sites

Brown-headed Cowbirds utilize the nests of a variety of birds at ACE Basin, Santee, and Mattamuskeet National Wildlife Refuges, and around Hartwell Lake.

FIELD NOTES The Brown-headed Cowbird flourishes throughout North America, adapting to newly cleared lands and exposing new songbirds—now more than 200 species—to its parasitic brooding habit. The female Brown-headed Cowbird lays up to 40 eggs a season in the nests of host birds, leaving the task of raising their young to the host species.

Year-round | Adult male

ORCHARD ORIOLE

Icterus spurius L 7¼" (18 cm)

FIELD MARKS

Male has black hood and upperparts, chestnut shoulders, rump, and underparts

Female olive above with black wings, yellowish below

Dark bill slightly decurved

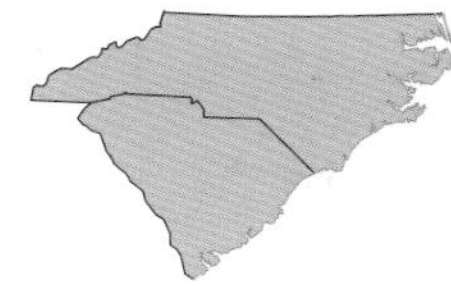

Behavior

Forages by inserting thin, sharply pointed bill into holes and crevices in trees and bushes. Hops from branch to branch fairly high up in trees. Males arrive at breeding ground before females and sing to attract mates. Courtship includes female drooping her wings and male bowing, repeatedly showing colors. Song is a loud, rapid burst of whistled notes, downslurred at end, which varies considerably from song to song. Call is sharp *chuck*.

Habitat

Locally common in suburban shade trees, open woodlands, and orchards. Female builds pouch-shaped nest in wooded areas, hung on branches too fragile to support many predators.

Local Sites

Orchard Orioles build their elaborate nests throughout the Carolinas. New River State Park is one good spot.

FIELD NOTES Named for the orange-and-black coat of arms of Lord Baltimore, the male Baltimore Oriole, *Icterus galbula* (inset), has similarly patterned plumage as the Orchard, but with chestnut areas replaced by bright orange. It breeds in the Appalachians and winters in the Carolinas' southern coastal regions.

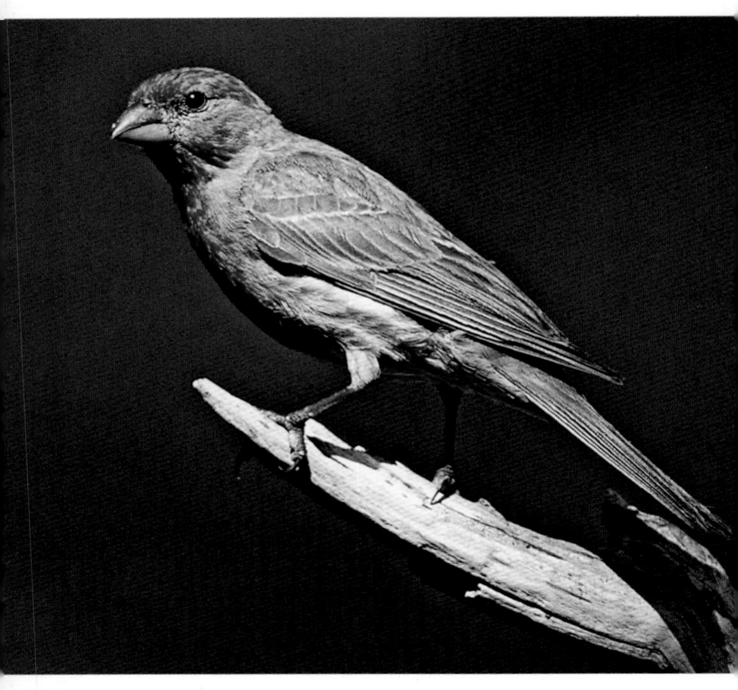

Year-round | Adult male

HOUSE FINCH

Carpodacus mexicanus L 6" (15 cm)

FIELD MARKS

Male's front of head, bib, and rump typically red, but can be orange or, occasionally, yellow

Brown streaked back, white belly, streaked flanks

Female streaked dusky brown on entire body

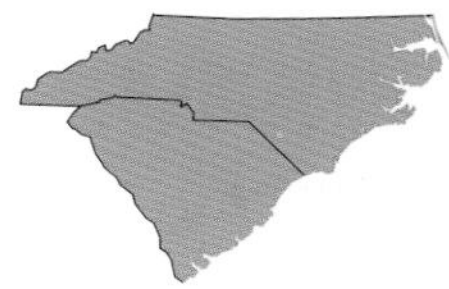

Behavior

A seed eater, the House Finch forages on the ground, in fields and in suburban yards. Often visits backyard feeders. Flies in undulating pattern, during which squared-off tail is evident. Male sings a conspicuously lively, high-pitched song consisting of varied three-note phrases, usually ending in a nasal *wheer.* Calls include a whistled *wheat.*

Habitat

Originally native to western U.S. and Central America, has adapted to varied habitats since introduction to the East Coast in 1940s. Prefers open areas, including suburban parks and areas where it can nest on buildings.

Local Sites

The House Finch is widespread year-round across the Carolinas. Look for it at feeders throughout the region and especially along the coast.

FIELD NOTES The Purple Finch, *Carpodacus purpureus,* is not purple but rose-red on the body of the adult male (inset, bottom). The female (inset, top) is gray-brown above and heavily streaked below, with a bolder face pattern and a more deeply notched tail than the House Finch. Look for both species throughout the Carolinas in winter.

Breeding | Adult male

AMERICAN GOLDFINCH

Carduelis tristis L 5" (13 cm)

FIELD MARKS

Breeding male bright yellow with black cap; female and winter male duller overall, lacking cap

Black wings have white bars

Black-and-white tail; white undertail coverts

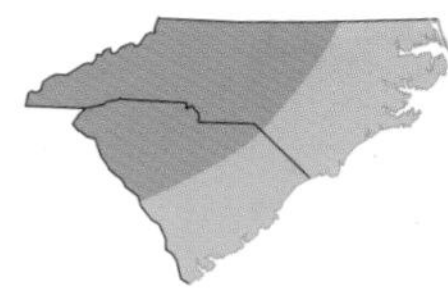

Behavior

Gregarious and active. Winter flocks may contain a hundred or more goldfinches and include several other species. The typical goldfinch diet, mostly seeds, is the most vegetarian of any North American bird; the goldfinch, however, sometimes eats insects as well. During courtship, male performs exaggerated, undulating aerial maneuvers, and often feeds the incubating female. Song is a lively series of trills, twitters, and *swee* notes. Distinctive flight call is *per-chik-o-ree.*

Habitat

Common but declining in weedy fields, open second-growth woodlands, and anywhere rich in thistles and sunflowers. Nests at edges of open areas or in old fields, often late in summer after thistles have bloomed so that the soft parts of the plant can be used as nest lining.

Local Sites

Carolina Sandhills National Wildlife Refuge, Hartwell Lake, and the Appalachian ridges are all good spots to look for the American Goldfinch year-round. It is also readily drawn to "thistle" feeders.

FIELD NOTES Sometimes a cowbird will lay its eggs in the nest of an American Goldfinch. Although the eggs will hatch, most young cowbirds die before they leave the nest, due to their inability to obtain enough protein from the finch's seed diet.

Breeding | Adult male

HOUSE SPARROW

Passer domesticus L 6¼" (16 cm)

FIELD MARKS

Breeding male has black bill, bib, and lores; chestnut nape, back, and shoulders

Winter male less distinct

Female has brown back, streaked with black; buffy eyestripe; and unstreaked grayish breast

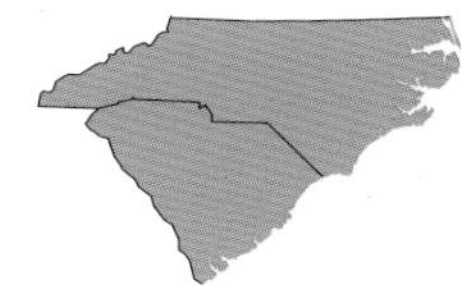

Behavior

Abundant and gregarious year-round. Hops around, feeding on grain, seeds, and shoots, or seeks out bird feeders for sunflower seeds and millet. In urban areas, begs for food from humans and will clean up any crumbs left behind. In spring and summer, multiple suitors will chase a possible mate in high-speed aerial pursuit. Females choose mate mostly according to song display. Singing males give persistent *cheep*.

Habitat

Found in close proximity to humans. Can be observed in urban and suburban areas and in rural landscapes inhabited by humans and livestock. Nests in any sheltered cavity, often usurping it from another species.

Local Sites

Abundant wherever humans reside, House Sparrows nest in even the most heavily urbanized areas.

FIELD NOTES Also known as the English Sparrow, the House Sparrow was first introduced into North America in New York's Central Park in the 1850s, an effort to populate the park with all the birds mentioned in Shakespeare's plays. It has since spread across the continent to become one of the most successful bird species in North America. Ironically, its numbers are declining precipitously in its native England.

Mostly Black

Mostly Black and White

Mostly Blue

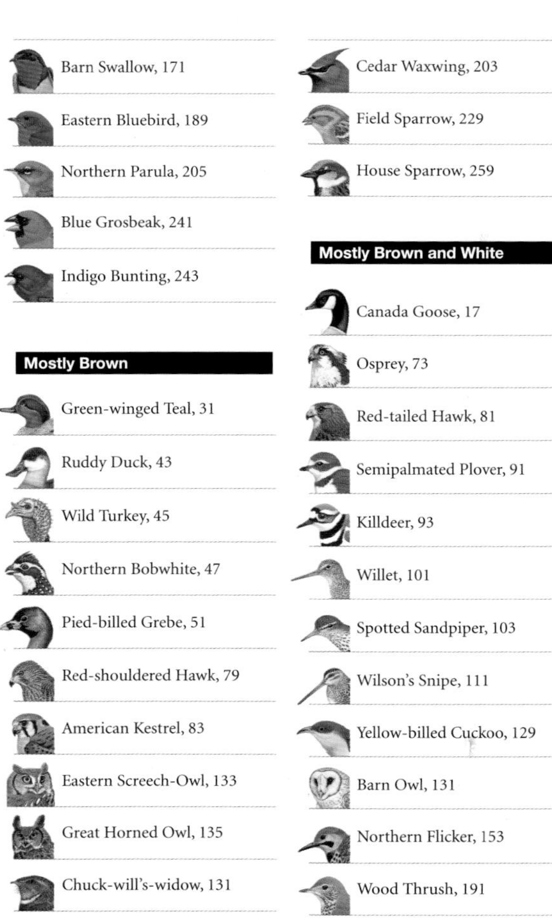

Mostly Brown

Mostly Brown and White

Mostly Gray

Mostly Greenish

Mostly Red

Mostly White

Mostly Yellow

Prominent Green Head

The main entry for each species is listed in **boldface** type and refers to the text page opposite the illustration.

A check-off box is provided next to each common-name entry so that you can use this index as a checklist of the species you have identified.

ACKNOWLEDGMENTS

The Book Division would like to thank the following photographers for their contributions in creating the *National Geographic Field Guide to Birds: The Carolinas*

Tom Vezo:

Tom Vezo is an award-winning wildlife photographer who is widely published throughout the U.S. and Europe. Located out of Green Valley, Arizona, he specializes in bird photography but photographs other wildlife and nature subjects as well. He is also a contributor to the *National Geographic Reference Atlas to the Birds of North America.* For a look at more of his images, find his gallery at tomvezo.com.

Brian E. Small:

Brian E. Small has been a full-time professional wildlife photographer specializing in birds for more than 15 years. In addition, he has been a regular columnist and Advisory Board member for *WildBird* magazine for the past 10 years. An avid naturalist and enthusiastic birder, Brian is currently the Photo Editor for the American Birding Association's *Birding* magazine. You can find more of his images at www.briansmallphoto.com.

Cortez C. Austin, Jr.:

Cortez Austin is a wildlife photographer who specializes in North American and tropical birds. He has a degree in zoology and has done graduate work in conservation, ecology, and microbiology. An ardent conservationist, he has donated images, given lectures, and written book reviews for conservation organizations. In addition he has published numerous articles and photographs in birding magazines in the United States. His photographs have also appeared in field guides, books, and brochures on wildlife.

Bates Littlehales:

National Geographic photographer for more than 30 years covering myriad subjects around the globe, Bates Littlehales continues to specialize in photographing birds and is an expert in capturing their beauty and ephemeral nature. Bates is co-author of the *National Geographic Photographic Field Guide: Birds,* and a contributor to the *National Geographic Reference Atlas to the Birds of North America.*

Larry Sansone:

An active birder since 1960, Larry Sansone began photographing wildlife in the early 1970s . His pictures are published in field guides and magazines in the U.S. and Europe. He was a technical advisor to the first edition of the *National Geographic Field Guide to the Birds of North America,* and he is photo editor of *Rare Birds of California* by the California Bird Records Committee.

ILLUSTRATIONS CREDITS

Photographs

Cortez C. Austin, Jr.: pp. 16, 18, 20, 54, 58, 92, 112, 122, 170, 202, 248. **Mike Danzenbaker**: p. 140. **Bates Littlehales**: pp. 134, 144, 150, 192, 214, 220, 224. **Larry Sansone**: pp. 102, 114, 208. **Brian E. Small**: pp. 12, 32, 34, 36, 40, 42, 52, 56, 62, 70, 72, 74, 78, 84, 90, 100, 104, 106, 108, 110, 118, 120, 124, 126, 128, 136, 144, 156, 158, 160, 172, 178, 180, 188, 190, 196, 198, 200, 212, 216, 218, 222, 226, 230, 232, 234, 238, 244, 254, 258. **Tom Vezo**: cover, pp. 2, 14, 22, 24, 26, 28, 30, 38, 44, 46, 48, 50, 60, 64, 66, 68, 76, 80, 82, 86, 88, 94, 96, 98, 116, 130, 132, 138, 146, 148, 152, 154, 162, 164, 166, 168, 174, 176, 182, 184, 186, 194, 204, 206, 210, 228, 236, 240, 242, 246, 250, 252, 256, 260.

Drawings

Jonathan Alderfer: pp. 10-Pacific Golden-Plover, 89, 109, 111, 127 (with Schmitt). **David Beadle**: p. 9. **Peter Burke**: pp. 67, 157, 221, 223, 225, 255. **Marc R. Hanson**: p. 87. **Cynthia J. House**: pp. 15, 17, 21, 25, 27, 31, 33, 37, 41. **H. Jon Janosik**: pp. 12, 53, 55, 97. **Donald L. Malick**: pp. 71, 73, 77, 83, 135, 147, 149, 153. **Kent Pendleton**: p. 45. **Diane Pierce**: pp. 10-Lark Sparrow, 59, 61, 63, 69, 231, 233, 241, 243, 257. **John C. Pitcher**: pp. 91, 99, 101. **H. Douglas Pratt**: pp. 129, 143, 155, 159, 161, 165, 169, 171, 177, 179, 185, 197, 207, 213, 247, 251. **David Quinn**: p. 49. **N. John Schmitt**: pp. 79, 127 (with Alderfer). **Thomas R. Schultz**: pp. 10-Great Black-backed Gull, 105, 113, 117, 119, 121, 191, 217.

NATIONAL GEOGRAPHIC FIELD GUIDE TO BIRDS: THE CAROLINAS

Edited by Jonathan Alderfer

Published by the National Geographic Society

John M. Fahey, Jr.,
President and Chief Executive Officer

Gilbert M. Grosvenor,
Chairman of the Board

Nina D. Hoffman,
Executive Vice President

Prepared by the Book Division

Kevin Mulroy,
Senior Vice President and Publisher

Kristin Hanneman, *Illustrations Director*

Marianne R. Koszorus, *Design Director*

Carl Mehler, *Director of Maps*

Barbara Brownell Grogan,
Executive Editor

Staff for this Book

Dan O'Toole, *Writer, Project Manager*

Megan McCarthy, *Designer*

Carol Norton, *Series Art Director*

Dan O'Toole, *Illustrations Editor*

Rachel Sweeney, *Illustrations Assistant*

Suzanne Poole, *Text Editor*

Matt Chwastyk, Sven Dolling,
Map Production

Rick Wain, *Production Project Manager*

Francis G. Koszorus, Michael Greninger,
Design Assistants

Manufacturing and Quality Control

Christopher A. Liedel,
Chief Financial Officer

Phillip L. Schlosser, *Managing Director*

John T. Dunn, *Technical Director*

One of the world's largest nonprofit scientific and educational organizations, the National Geographic Society was founded in 1888 "for the increase and diffusion of geographic knowledge." Fulfilling this mission, the Society educates and inspires millions every day through its magazines, books, television programs, videos, maps and atlases, research grants, the National Geographic Bee, teacher workshops, and innovative classroom materials. The Society is supported through membership dues, charitable gifts, and income from the sale of its educational products. This support is vital to National Geographic's mission to increase global understanding and promote conservation of our planet through exploration, research, and education.

For more information, please call 1-800-NGS LINE (647-5463) or write to the following address:

National Geographic Society
1145 17th Street N.W.
Washington, D.C. 20036-4688 U.S.A.

Visit the Society's Web site at www.nationalgeographic.com.

Library of Congress Cataloging-in-Publication Data

National Geographic field guide to birds. Carolinas / edited by Jonathan Alderfer.

p. cm., ISBN 0-7922-4186-X

1. Birds--North Carolina--Identification.
2. Birds--South Carolina--Identification.
I. Title: Field guide to birds. Carolinas. II. Alderfer, Jonathan K. III. NGS. (U.S.)

QL684.N8N38 2005

598'.09756--dc2   22005050290